A Close-Knit Family

A Close-Knit Family

Sweaters for Everyone You Love

Melissa Leapman

Photographs by Jack Deutsch

Publisher: Jim Childs

Acquisitions Editor: Jolynn Gower

Assistant Editor: Sarah Coe

Technical Editor: Carla Patrick Scott

Copy Editor: Candace B. Levy

Designer: Maria L. Miller

Layout Artist: Maria L. Miller

Photographer: Jack Deutsch

Illustrator: Rosalie Vacarro

Taunton
BOOKS & VIDEOS
for fellow enthusiasts

Printed in the United States of America
10 9 8 7 6 5 4 3 2 1

The Taunton Press, Inc.,
63 South Main Street, PO Box 5506,
Newtown, CT 06470-5506
e-mail: tp@taunton.com

Distributed by Publishers Group West

Library of Congress Cataloging-in-Publication Data

Leapman, Melissa.
    A close-knit family: sweaters for everyone you love / Melissa
Leapman; photographs by Jack Deutsch.
        p.   cm.
        ISBN 1–56158–251–4
        1. Knitting Patterns. 2. Sweaters. I. Title.
TT825.L385   1999
746.43'20432—dc21   99–14825
                                                           CIP

For Mother and Father

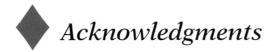 ## *Acknowledgments*

I wish to thank the following knitters for their hard work and enthusiasm while creating the garments for this book: Joyce Bischoff, Helen Borga, Ellen Bray, Peggy Dailey, Pat Geiger, Leanne Gray, Cheryl Keeley, Nancy Maakestad, Maggie McManus, Viola Oldland, Eleanor Swogger, and Scarlet Taylor.

Special thanks to my wonderful assistant, JoAnn Moss, for her help in preparing the sweaters and patterns, and to Ann Smith, for her friendship and advice.

I am indebted to the yarn and button companies who generously supplied materials for this book. They, along with many magazine editors in the needlework industry, have supported my designs throughout my career.

I am grateful to Michael Blowney, whose encouragement enabled me to both start and complete this exciting project.

The editors would like to express thanks to our wonderful volunteer models and their parents, who generously gave us their time and patience: Charlotte and Wyl Chapman, William Culpepper, Hannah Delohery, Charlotte Ehrhardt, Alexandra Kandiew, Tessa Plummer, Stephen Rahr, Jessie and Gena Rochler, Will Roman, Molly and Daniel Sheehan, Charlie Smart, and Emilie and Jamie Worth.

 # Contents

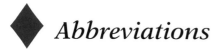

Abbreviations

approx	approximately		P1 (or P2)	purl 1 st (or purl 2 sts)
beg	begin(ning)		patt(s)	pattern(s)
BO	bind off		psso	pass slipped st over
ch	chain		p2sso	pass 2 slipped st over
cm	centimeter(s)		rem	remain(s)(ing)
cn	cable needle		RH	right hand
CO	cast on		rnd(s)	round(s)
cont	continu(e)(ing)		RS	right side(s)
dec	decreas(e)(ing)		sc	single crochet
g	gram(s)		ssk	slip 1 st as if to knit, slip another st as if to knit, then knit these 2 sts together
inc	increas(e)(ing)			
k2tog	knit two sts together			
K1 (or K2)	knit 1 st (or knit 2 sts)		st(s)	stitch(es)
LH	left hand		tog	together
m	meter(s)		WS	wrong side(s)
mm	millimeter(s)		yds	yards
oz	ounce(s)			
p2tog	purl two sts together		*	repeat from * as many times as indicated

◆ *Introduction*

Let's face it: As knitters, we rarely knit just for ourselves. We enjoy knitting for others. In this book, I have put together a collection of designs to please *everybody* on your list, including, for those lucky occasions, yourself!

Each section presents a basic theme such as Fair Isle, ribs, or cables and offers variations for different members of the family. Sweaters in a his and hers set, for example, might feature common elements, such as braided cable panels or textured rib patterns; but the sweaters are not identical. In The South Hadley Tweeds, for example, the woman's version has a fitted, shaped silhouette, whereas the man's is oversized and boxy.

Similarly, the family ensembles consist of coordinating sweaters rather than adult sweaters with miniaturized duplicates for children. In the Nordic Warmth set, for instance, allover Fair Isle stripes in such high-contrast colors might overwhelm a child; little Fair Isle borders, however, look great finishing off the more subtly patterned sweater.

By not merely reworking the same sweater in many different sizes, these projects will keep even the most prolific knitter engaged. Spend your precious knitting time creating sweaters for your family that are sometimes quick and easy, sometimes a little more challenging, but always, I hope, interesting and fun.

Entwined Hearts

These three sweaters feature twisted knit
stitches that travel to create little heart motifs.
In both the woman's and infant's versions,
these hearts are filled with Seed Stitch.
For a more subtle pattern, the Seed Stitch
is omitted from the man's pullover.

Woman's High-Neck Pullover

Skill Level
Intermediate

Sizes
Woman's Small (Medium, Large). Instructions are for smallest size, with changes for other sizes noted in parentheses as necessary.

Finished Measurements
Bust: 39 (44½, 50)"/99 (113, 127) cm
Length: 24 (25, 26)"/61 (63.5, 66) cm
Sleeve width at upper arm: 18 (19, 20)"/45.5 (48.5, 51) cm

Materials
- Brown Sheep's *Naturespun Worsted* (worsted weight; 100% wool; 3½ oz/100 g; approx 245 yds/224 m), 8 (8, 9) skeins Victorian Pink #N87
- Knitting needles, sizes 6 and 7 (4 and 4.5 mm) or size needed to obtain gauge
- Two stitch holders

Gauge
With larger needles in Seed St Heart Patt, 23 sts and 33 rows = 4"/10 cm. **To save time, take time to check gauge.**

Twisted K2 P2 Rib Patt (multiple of 4 sts plus 2 sts)
Row 1 (RS): K2 through back loop, *P2, K2 through back loop. Repeat from * across.
Row 2: P2, *K2, P2 through back loop. Repeat from * across.
Repeat Rows 1 and 2 for patt.

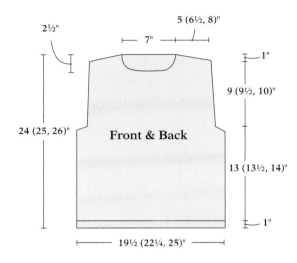

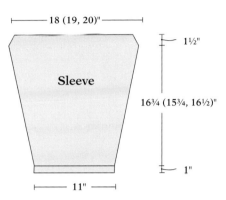

Back

With smaller needles, CO 114 (130, 146) sts. Work Twisted K2 P2 Rib Patt for 1"/2.5 cm, ending after WS row. Change to larger needles, beg and end where indicated, and work even in Seed St Heart Patt until piece measures 14 (14½, 15)"/35.5 (37, 38) cm from beg.

Shape Armholes: BO 3 sts at beg of next two rows, then dec 1 st each side every other row five times—98 (114, 130) sts rem. Work even until armholes measure 9 (9½, 10)"/23 (24, 25.5) cm.

Shape Shoulders: BO 7 (9, 11) sts at beg of next six rows, then BO 8 (10, 12) sts at beg of next two rows. Slip rem 40 sts onto holder for back of neck.

Front

Work same as back until the armholes measure 7½ (8, 8½)"/19 (20.5, 21.5) cm.

Shape Neck: Work across first 42 (50, 58) sts, slip middle 14 sts onto holder for front of neck; join second skein of yarn and work to end of row. Work both sides at once with separate skeins of yarn, and BO 3 sts each neck edge twice, BO 2 sts each neck edge twice, then dec 1 st each neck edge every other row three times; **and at the same time,** when front measures same as back to shoulders, **Shape Shoulders** same as for back.

Sleeves

With smaller needles, CO 66 sts. Work Twisted K2 P2 Rib Patt for 1"/2.5 cm, ending after WS row. Change to larger needles, beg and end where indicated, and beg Seed St Heart Patt. Inc 1 st each side on next row and then every fourth row 0 (1, 8) more times, then every sixth row 8 (20, 16) times, then every eighth row 10 (0, 0) times—104 (110, 116) sts. Cont even until sleeve measures 17¾ (16¾ , 17½)"/45 (42.5, 44.5) cm from beg.

Shape Cap: Work same as for back armhole shaping. BO the rem 88 (94, 100) sts.

Finishing

Sew left shoulder seam.

Neckband: With RS facing, pick up and knit 98 sts around neckline, including sts from neck holders. Work rnds of Twisted K2 P2 Rib Patt for 3"/7.5 cm. BO **loosely** in rib.

Sew right shoulder seam, including side of neckband. Set in sleeves. Sew sleeve and side seams.

Seed Stitch Heart Patt

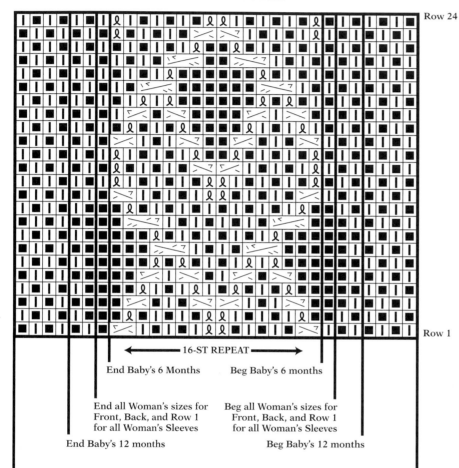

Row 24

Row 1

← 16-ST REPEAT →

End Baby's 6 Months   Beg Baby's 6 months

End all Woman's sizes for   Beg all Woman's sizes for
Front, Back, and Row 1   Front, Back, and Row 1
for all Woman's Sleeves   for all Woman's Sleeves

End Baby's 12 months   Beg Baby's 12 months

End Baby's 18 months   Beg Baby's 18 months

Designer Hint

To make the pattern stand out clearly,
be sure to work *into the back loop*
of each twisted stitch
on both **RS** and **WS** rows.

Key

I = Knit on RS; purl on WS

■ = Purl on RS; knit on WS

Ջ = Knit through back loop on RS; purl through back loop on WS

= Slip next st to cn and hold in **FRONT** of work; purl next st; knit stitch from cn through back loop

= Slip next st to cn and hold in **BACK** of work; knit next st through back loop; purl st from cn

= Slip next st to cn and hold in **BACK** of work; knit next st through back loop; knit st from cn

= Slip next st to cn and hold in **FRONT** of work; knit next st; knit st from cn through back loop

= Slip next 2 sts to cn and hold in **BACK** of work; knit next st through back loop; purl first st from cn; knit next st from cn

= Slip next st to cn and hold in **FRONT** of work; purl next st; knit next st; knit st from cn through back loop

Man's V-Neck Pullover

Man's V-Neck Pullover

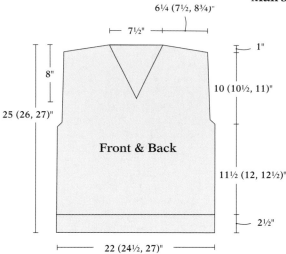

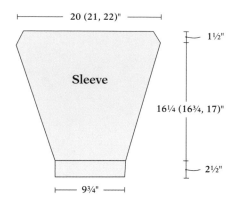

Skill Level
Intermediate

Sizes
Man's Small (Medium, Large). Instructions are for smallest size, with changes for other sizes noted in parentheses as necessary.

Finished Measurements
Chest: 44 (49, 54)"/112 (124.5, 137) cm
Length: 25 (26, 27)"/63.5 (66, 68.5) cm
Sleeve width at upper arm: 20 (21, 22)"/51 (53.5, 56) cm

Materials
- Brown Sheep's *Naturespun Worsted* (worsted weight; 100% wool; 3½ oz/100 g; approx 245 yds/224 m), 9 (10, 10) skeins Winter Blue #117
- Knitting needles, sizes 5 and 7 (3.75 and 4.5 mm) or size needed to obtain gauge
- 16"/40 cm circular knitting needle, size 5 (3.75 mm)
- Two stitch holders

Gauge
With larger needles in Reverse Stockinette Heart Patt, 26 sts and 32 rows = 4"/10 cm. **To save time, take time to check gauge.**

Twisted K2 P2 Rib Patt
Same as for Woman's High-Neck Pullover

Back
With smaller needles, CO 146 (162, 178) sts. Work Twisted K2 P2 Rib Patt for 2 ½"/6.5 cm, ending after WS row. Change to larger needles, beg and end where indicated, and work even in Reverse Stockinette Heart Patt until piece measures 14 (14½, 15)"/35.5 (37, 38) cm from beg.
Shape Armholes: BO 3 sts at beg of next two rows, then dec 1 st each side every other row five times—130 (146, 162) sts rem. Work even until armholes measure 10 (10½, 11)"/25.5 (26.5, 28) cm.
Shape Shoulders: BO 10 (12, 14) sts at beg of next six rows, then BO 11 (13, 15) sts at beg of next two rows. Slip rem 48 sts onto holder for back of neck.

Front
Work same as back until armholes measure 3 (3½, 4)"/7.5 (9, 10) cm.
Shape Neck: Work across first 63 (71, 79) sts, k2tog, join second skein of yarn and ssk, work to end row. Work both sides at once with separate skeins of yarn, and dec 1 st each neck edge every other row seventeen times, then every fourth row six times; **and at the same time,** when front measures same as back to shoulders, **Shape Shoulders** same as for back.

Sleeves
With smaller needles, CO 66 sts. Work Twisted K2 P2 Rib Patt for 2½"/6.5 cm, ending after WS row. Change to larger needles, beg and end where indicated, and beg Reverse Stockinette Heart Patt. Inc 1 st each side on next row, and then every other row 2 (8, 13) more times, then every fourth row 29 (27, 25) times—130 (138, 144) sts. Cont even until sleeve measures 18¾ (19¼, 19½)"/47.5 (49, 49.5) cm from beg.

Reverse Stockinette Heart Patt

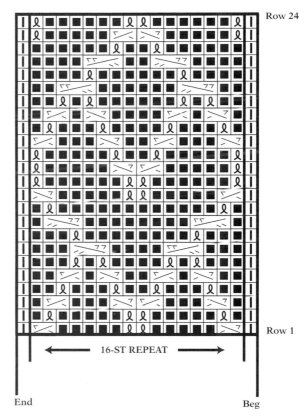

Row 24

Row 1

← 16-ST REPEAT →

End

Beg

Shape Cap: Work same as for back armhole shaping. BO rem 114 (122, 128) sts.

Finishing
Sew shoulder seams.

Neckband: With RS facing and circular knitting needle, beg at left shoulder neck edge, pick up and knit 56 sts evenly along left front neck to center front, place marker, pick up and knit 56 sts evenly along right front neck edge, knit 48 sts from back neck holder—160 sts total. Work in Twisted K2 P2 Rib Patt until 2 sts before marker, ssk, slip marker, k2tog, work Twisted K2 P2 Rib Patt to end rnd. Cont in patt as established, dec 1 st before and after marker every rnd. When band measures 1"/2.5 cm, BO **loosely** in rib.

Set in sleeves. Sew sleeve and side seams.

Key

I	= Knit on RS; purl on WS
■	= Purl on RS; knit on WS
ℓ	= Knit through back loop on RS; purl through back loop on WS
⟋⟍	= Slip next st to cn and hold in BACK of work; knit next st through back loop; purl st from cn
⟍⟋	= Slip next st to cn and hold in FRONT of work; purl next st; knit st from cn through back loop
⟋⟍	= Slip next 2 sts to cn and hold in BACK of work; knit next st through back loop; purl 2 sts from cn
⟍⟋	= Slip next st to cn and hold in FRONT of work; purl next 2 sts; knit st from cn through back loop

Baby's Pullover and Pants Set

Skill Level
Intermediate

Sizes
Infant's 6 (12, 18) months. Instructions are for smallest size, with changes for other sizes noted in parentheses as necessary.

Finished Measurements
Pullover chest: 22 (24, 27)"/56 (61, 68.5) cm
Pullover length: 10 (11, 12½)"/25.5 (28, 32) cm
Sleeve width at upper arm: 9 (10, 10½)"/23 (25.5, 26.5) cm
Pants length: 15 (16, 17)"/38 (40.5, 43) cm

Materials
- Brown Sheep's *Naturespun Worsted* (worsted weight; 100% wool; 3½ oz/100 g; approx 245 yds/224 m), 4 (5, 6) skeins Platte River Blue #N64
- Knitting needles, sizes 6 and 7 (4 and 4.5 mm) or size needed to obtain gauge
- 16"/40 cm circular knitting needle, size 6 (4 mm)
- Two stitch holders
- Four ½"/15 mm buttons (JHB International's *Moonstone* style #71623 in White was used on sample garment)
- 1"/2.5 cm wide elastic measured to fit baby's waist

Gauge
With larger needles in Seed St Heart Patt, 23 sts and 33 rows = 4"/10 cm. **To save time, take time to check gauge.**

Twisted K2 P2 Rib Patt
Same as for Woman's High-Neck Pullover

Seed St Rib Patt (multiple of 8 sts)
Row 1 (RS): *K1 through back loop, P2, (K1, P1) twice, K1 through back loop. Repeat from * across.
Row 2: *P1 through back loop, K2, (P1, K1) twice, P1 through back loop. Repeat from * across.
Repeat Rows 1 and 2 for patt.

Pullover Back
With smaller needles, CO 66 (70, 78) sts. Work Twisted K2 P2 Rib Patt for 1"/2.5 cm, dec 2 (0, 0) sts on last row—64 (70, 78) sts. Change to larger needles, beg and end where indicated, and work Seed St Heart Patt until piece measures 10 (11, 12½)"/25.5 (28, 32) cm from beg, ending after WS row. Next Row: BO 44 (50, 54) sts, and slip rem 20 (20, 34) sts onto holder.

Baby's Pullover and Pants Set

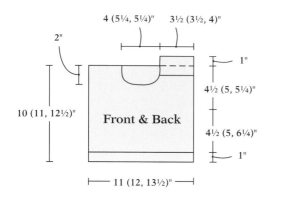

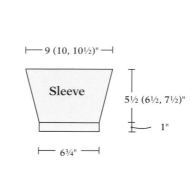

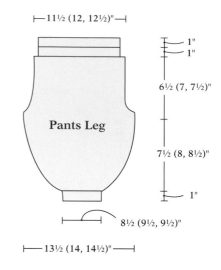

Pullover Front

Work same as back until piece measures 8 (9, 10½)"/20.5 (23, 27) cm from beg, ending after WS row.
Shape Neck: Work across first 27 (29, 33) sts, slip middle 10 (12, 12) sts onto holder for front of neck; join second skein of yarn and work to end of row. Work both sides at once with separate skeins of yarn, and BO 4 (5, 5) sts each neck edge once, BO 2 (3, 3) sts each neck edge once, then dec 1 st each neck edge once. Next Row (RS): Work even. Next Row (WS): Work across first 20 (20, 24) sts, slip rem sts onto holder for left shoulder. Cont even in patt on first group of sts until piece measures 10 (11, 12½)"/25.5 (28, 32) cm from beg. BO.

Pullover Sleeves

With smaller needles, CO 42 sts. Work Twisted K2 P2 Rib Patt for 1"/2.5 cm, dec 2 sts on last row—40 sts. Change to larger needles, and beg Seed St Rib Patt. Inc 1 st each side every fourth row 3 (5, 8) times, then every sixth row 4 (4, 3) times—54 (58, 62) sts. Cont even until sleeve measures 6½ (7½, 8½)"/16.5 (19, 21.5) cm from beg. BO.

Pullover Finishing

Sew right shoulder seam.
Neckband: With circular knitting needle, pick up and knit 54 (58, 58) sts around neckline, including sts from front neck holder. Work rows of Twisted K2 P2 Rib Patt for 1"/2.5 cm. BO in rib.
Button Band: With RS facing and smaller needles, pick up and knit 6 sts along side of neckband, then pick up and knit 20 (20, 24) sts from left back shoulder holder—26 (26, 30) sts. Work Twisted K2 P2 Rib Patt until band measures 1"/2.5 cm from beg. BO in rib. Place markers for four evenly spaced buttons along button band.
Buttonhole Band: With RS facing and smaller needles, pick up and knit 20 (20, 24) sts from shoulder holder, then pick up and knit 6 sts along side of neckband—26 (26, 30) sts total. Work Twisted K2 P2 Rib Patt until band measures ½"/1.5 cm. Next Row: Make buttonholes opposite markers by working (k2tog, yarn over). Cont in Twisted K2 P2 Rib Patt as established until band measures 1"/2.5 cm. BO in rib.

Overlap buttonhole band over button band and sew armhole ends tog. Place markers 4½ (5, 5¼)"/11.5 (12.5, 13.5) cm down from shoulders. Set in sleeves between markers. Sew sleeve and side seams. Sew on buttons.

Pants Legs (Make Two)

With smaller needles, CO 48 (56, 56) sts. Work Twisted Rib Patt working Row 1 as follows: *knit 1 st through back loop, purl 2 sts, knit 1 st through back loop; repeat from * to end. Cont as established for 1"/2.5 cm. Change to larger needles, and beg Seed St Rib Patt. Inc 1 st each side every other row 10 (2, 2) times, then every fourth row 6 (11, 12) times—80 (82, 84) sts. Cont even until piece measures 8½ (9, 9½)"/21.5 (23, 24) cm from beg.

Shape Crotch: BO 2 sts at beg of next two rows, then dec 1 st each side every other row 4 (2, 0) times, then every fourth row 1 (2, 4) times—66 (70, 72) sts. Cont even until piece measures 15 (16, 17)"/38 (40.5, 43) cm from beg. Place sts onto holder.

Pants Finishing

Sew inside leg seams. Sew center front and back seams.

Waistband: With RS facing and circular knitting needle, pick up and knit sts from leg holders. Join and work rnds of Twisted K2 P2 Rib Patt for 1"/2.5 cm. Next Rnd (turning ridge): Purl around. Cont in Twisted K2 P2 Rib Patt for 1"/2.5 cm more. BO. Fold waistband in half to WS at turning ridge, and sew into place to form casing, leaving opening for elastic. Cut elastic to fit waist with ½"/1.5 cm overlap. Slip elastic through casing, and sew ends tog securely. Sew casing closed.

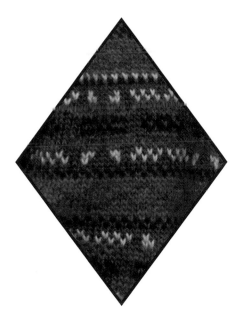

Spicy
Fair Isles

In this family trio, a warm, curry-inspired color palette enlivens familiar Fair Isle motifs. Contemporary styling details such as the chunky zipper or rolled edges make these updated classics fun to wear.

Woman's Rolled-Neck Pullover

◆

Designer Hint

To minimize tangles at the end of each Fair Isle row, alternate between picking up one color from beneath the other and one color from above the other across the row.

◆

Skill Level

Intermediate

Sizes

Woman's Small (Medium, Large, Extra-Large). Instructions are for smallest size, with changes for other sizes noted in parentheses as necessary.

Finished Measurements

Bust: 39 (42, 45, 48)"/99 (106.5, 114.5, 122) cm

Length: 20 (20, 21, 22)"/51 (51, 53.5, 56) cm

Sleeve width at upper arm: 17 (18, 19, 20)"/43 (45.5, 48.5, 51) cm

Materials

• Classic Elite's *Montera* (heavy worsted weight; 50% llama/50% wool, 3½ oz/100 g; approx 127 yds/114 m), 4 (4, 4, 5) hanks Quechua Tangerine #3806 **(A)**; 2 (2, 2, 3) hanks Calamarca Rose #3861

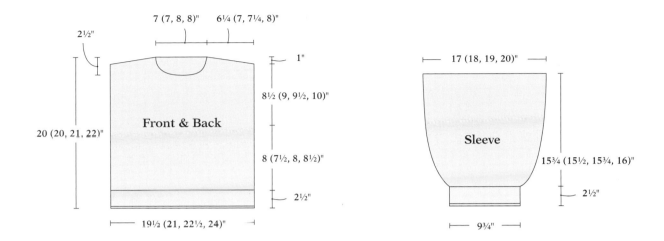

Front & Back dimensions:
2½"
7 (7, 8, 8)"   6¼ (7, 7¼, 8)"
1"
8½ (9, 9½, 10)"
20 (20, 21, 22)"
8 (7½, 8, 8½)"
2½"
19½ (21, 22½, 24)"

Sleeve dimensions:
17 (18, 19, 20)"
15¾ (15½, 15¾, 16)"
2½"
9¾"

(B); 3 (4, 4, 4) hanks Lima Green #3881 **(C)**; and 1 (1, 1, 2) hank San Isidro Gold #3809 **(D)**

- Knitting needles, sizes 8 and 9 (5 and 5.5 mm) or size needed to obtain gauge
- Two stitch holders

Gauge
With larger needles in Woman's Fair Isle Patt, 18 sts and 20 rows = 4"/10 cm. **To save time, take time to check gauge.**

Back
With smaller needles and A, CO 89 (95, 103, 109) sts. Beg with a purl row, work seven rows of Stockinette St. Next Row (RS): Change to larger needles, and work K1 P1 rib until piece measures 2½"/6.5 cm from beg, allowing edge to curl, ending after RS row. Next Row (WS): Purl across. Beg and end Woman's Fair Isle Patt where indicated, and work even until piece measures 19 (19, 20, 21)"/48.5 (48.5, 51, 53.5) cm from beg.

Shape Shoulders: BO 10 (11, 11, 12) sts at beg of next four rows, then BO 9 (10, 12, 13) sts at beg of next two rows. Slip rem 31 (31, 35, 35) sts onto holder for back of neck.

Front
Work same as for back until piece measures 17½ (17½, 18½, 19½)"/44.5 (44.5, 47, 49.5) cm from beg.
Shape Neck: Work across first 38 (41, 44, 47) sts, slip middle 13 (13, 15, 15) sts onto holder for front of neck; join second ball of yarn, and work to end row. Work both sides at once with separate balls of yarn, and BO 3 sts each neck edge once (once, twice, twice), BO 2 sts each neck edge twice (twice, once, once), then dec 1 st each neck edge every row twice; **and at the same time,** when front measures same as back to shoulders, **Shape Shoulders** same as for back.

Sleeves
With smaller needles and A, CO 45 sts. Beg with a purl row, work seven rows of Stockinette St. Next Row (RS): Change to larger needles, and work K1 P1 rib until piece measures 2½"/6.5 cm from beg, allowing edge to curl, ending

after RS row. Next Row (WS): Purl across. Beg and end Woman's Fair Isle Patt where indicated, and inc 1 st each side every other row 0 (0, 2, 7) times, then every fourth row 10 (16, 18, 16) times, then every sixth row 6 (2, 0, 0) times—77 (81, 85, 91) sts. Work even until sleeve measures 18¼ (18, 18¼, 18½)"/46.5 (46, 46.5, 47) cm from the beg. BO.

Finishing
Sew left shoulder seam.
Neckband: With RS facing, larger needles, and A, pick up and knit 72 (72, 78, 78) sts around neckline, including sts from neck holders. Work K1 P1 rib for 2"/5 cm, ending after WS row. Change to smaller needles, and work seven rows of Stockinette St. BO **loosely.**
Sew right shoulder seam, including side of neckband. Place markers 8½ (9, 9½, 10)"/21.5 (23, 24, 25.5) cm down from shoulders. Set in sleeves between markers. Sew sleeve and side seams.

Woman's Fair Isle Patt

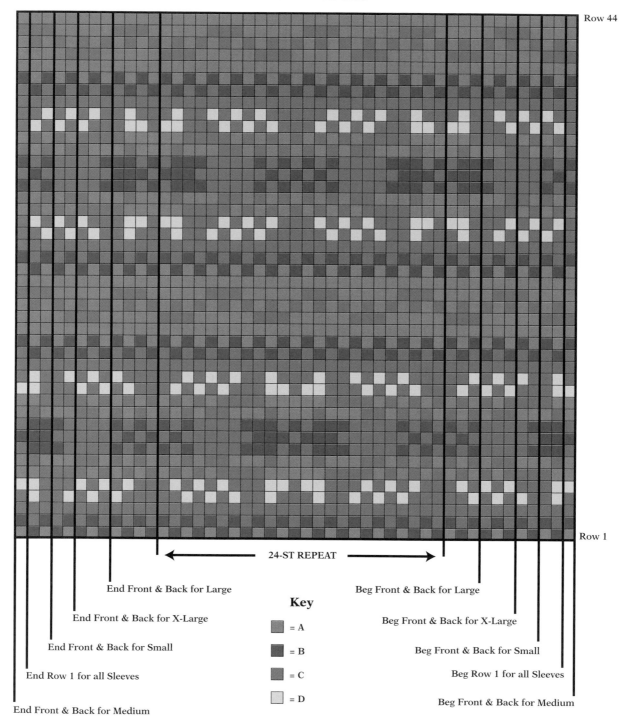

Row 44

Row 1

24-ST REPEAT

End Front & Back for Large

End Front & Back for X-Large

End Front & Back for Small

End Row 1 for all Sleeves

End Front & Back for Medium

Beg Front & Back for Large

Beg Front & Back for X-Large

Beg Front & Back for Small

Beg Row 1 for all Sleeves

Beg Front & Back for Medium

Key

■ = A

■ = B

■ = C

□ = D

Man's Crew-Neck Pullover

Skill Level
Intermediate

Sizes
Man's Small (Medium, Large, Extra-Large). Instructions are for smallest size, with changes for other sizes noted in parentheses as necessary.

Finished Measurements
Chest: 44 (48, 52, 56)"/112 (122, 132, 142) cm
Length: 27 (28, 28, 29)"/68.5 (71, 71, 73.5) cm
Sleeve width at upper arm: 20 (21, 22, 23)"/51 (53.5, 56, 58.5) cm

Materials
- Classic Elite's *Montera* (heavy worsted weight; 50% llama/50% wool, 3½ oz/100 g; approx 127 yds/114 m), 5 (5, 6, 7) hanks Bolsita Orange #3885 (**A**); 2 (2, 3, 3) hanks Basilico #3842 (**B**); 5 (5, 6, 7) hanks Sierra Moss #3897 (**C**); and 1 (1, 2, 2) hank San Isidro Gold #3809 (**D**)
- Knitting needles, size 9 (5.5 mm) or size needed to obtain gauge
- 16"/40 cm circular knitting needle, size 8 (5 mm)
- Two stitch holders

Gauge
In Man's Fair Isle Patt, 18 sts and 20 rows = 4"/10 cm. **To save time, take time to check gauge.**

Man's Fair Isle Patt

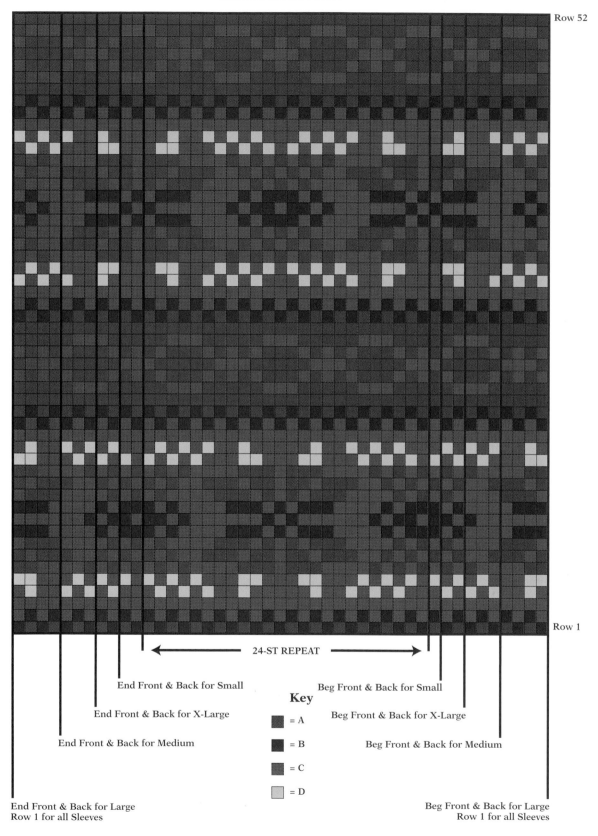

Row 52

Row 1

24-ST REPEAT

End Front & Back for Small

End Front & Back for X-Large

End Front & Back for Medium

End Front & Back for Large
Row 1 for all Sleeves

Beg Front & Back for Small

Beg Front & Back for X-Large

Beg Front & Back for Medium

Beg Front & Back for Large
Row 1 for all Sleeves

Key

■ = A

■ = B

■ = C

■ = D

Man's Crew-Neck Pullover

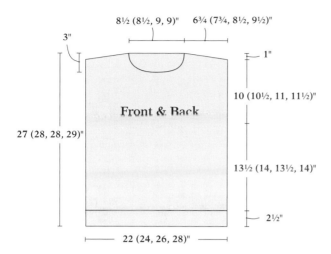

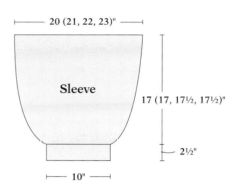

Back

With A, CO 99 (109, 117, 127) sts. Work K1 P1 rib until piece measures 2½"/6.5 cm from beg, ending after RS row. Next Row (WS): Purl across. Beg and end Man's Fair Isle Patt where indicated, and work even until piece measures 26 (27, 27, 28)"/66 (68.5, 68.5, 71) cm from beg.

Shape Shoulders: BO 10 (12, 13, 14) sts at beg of next four rows, then BO 10 (11, 12, 15) sts at beg of next two rows. Slip rem 39 (39, 41, 41) sts onto holder for back of neck.

Front

Work same as back until piece measures 24 (25, 25, 26)"/61 (63.5, 63.5, 66) cm from beg.

Shape Neck: Work across first 42 (47, 50, 55) sts, slip middle 15 (15, 17, 17) sts onto holder for front of neck; join second ball of yarn, and work to end of row. Work both sides at once with separate balls of yarn, and BO 4 sts each neck edge once, BO 3 sts each neck edge once, BO 2 sts each neck edge once, then dec 1 st each neck edge every row three times; **and at the same time,** when front measures same as back to shoulders, **Shape Shoulders** same as for back.

Sleeves

With A, CO 45 sts. Work K1 P1 rib until piece measures 2½"/6.5 cm from beg, ending after RS row. Next Row (WS): Purl across. Beg and end Man's Fair Isle Patt where indicated, and inc 1 st each side every other row 6 (10, 13, 17) times, then every fourth row 17 (15, 14, 12) times—91 (95, 99, 103) sts. Cont even until sleeve measures 19½ (19½, 20, 20)"/49.5 (49.5, 51, 51) cm from beg. BO.

Finishing

Sew shoulder seams.

Neckband: With RS facing, circular knitting needle, and A, pick up and knit 94 (94, 98, 98) sts around neckline, including sts from neck holders. Work rnds of K1 P1 rib for 1"/2.5 cm. BO in rib.

Place markers 10 (10½, 11, 11½)"/25.5 (26.5, 28, 29) cm down from shoulders. Set in sleeves between markers. Sew sleeve and side seams.

Child's Zippered Pullover

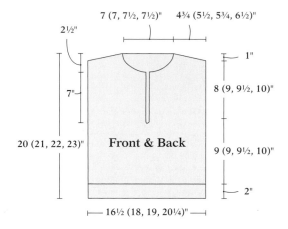

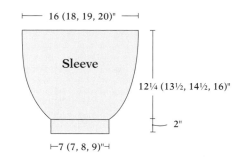

Skill Level
Intermediate

Sizes
Child's 8 (10, 12, 14). Instructions are for smallest size, with changes for other sizes noted in parentheses as necessary.

Finished Measurements
Chest: 33 (36, 38, 40½)"/84 (91.5, 96.5, 103) cm

Length: 20 (21, 22, 23)"/51 (53.5, 56, 58.5) cm

Sleeve width at upper arm: 16 (18, 19, 20)"/40.5 (45.5, 48.5, 51) cm

Materials
- Classic Elite's *Montera* (heavy worsted weight; 50% llama/50% wool, 3½ oz/100 g; approx 127 yds/114 m), 3 (3, 3, 4) hanks Quechua Tangerine #3806 (**A**); 2 (2, 2, 3) hanks Cintachi Red #3858 (**B**); 3 (3, 4, 4) hanks Sierra Moss #3897 (**C**); and 1 (1, 1, 2) hank San Isidro Gold #3809 (**D**)
- Knitting needles, sizes 8 and 9 (5 and 5.5 mm) or size needed to obtain gauge
- One stitch holder
- 7"/18 cm zipper

Gauge
With larger needles in Child's Fair Isle Patt, 18 sts and 20 rows = 4"/10 cm. **To save time, take time to check gauge.**

Back
With smaller needles and A, CO 77 (83, 89, 93) sts. Work K1 P1 rib for 2"/5 cm. Next Row (WS): Change to larger needles, and purl across. Beg and end Child's Fair Isle Patt where indicated, and work even until piece measures 19 (20, 21, 22)"/48.5 (51, 53.5, 56) cm from beg.

Shape Shoulders: BO 8 (9, 9, 10) sts at beg of next four rows, then BO 7 (8, 10, 10) sts at beg of next two rows. Slip rem 31 (31, 33, 33) sts onto holder for back of neck.

Front
Work same as for back until piece measures 10½ (11½, 12½, 13½)"/26.5 (29, 31.5, 34) cm from beg.

Divide for Zipper Opening: Work across first 37 (40, 43, 45) sts, slip middle 3 sts onto holder or safety pin; join second ball of yarn and work to end row. Work even on both sides at once with separate balls of yarn until piece measures 17½ (18½, 19½, 20½)"/44.5 (47, 49.5, 52) cm from beg.

Shape Neck: BO 5 (5, 6, 6) sts each neck edge once, BO 3 sts each neck edge once, BO 2 sts each neck edge twice, then dec 1 st each neck edge every row twice; **and at the same time,** when front measures same as back to shoulders, **Shape Shoulders** same as for back.

Sleeves
With smaller needles and A, CO 31 (31, 37, 41) sts. Work K1 P1 rib for 2"/5 cm. Next Row (WS): Change to larger

needles, and purl across. Beg and end Child's Fair Isle Patt where indicated, and inc 1 st each side every other row 14 (19, 17, 13) times, then every fourth row 7 (6, 8, 12) times—73 (81, 87, 91) sts. Work even until sleeve measures 14¼ (15½, 16½, 18)"/36 (39.5, 42, 45.5) cm from beg. BO.

Finishing

Sew shoulder seams.

Collar: With RS facing, smaller needles, and A, pick up and knit 71 (71, 75, 75) sts around neckline, including sts from back neck holder. Work K1 P1 rib for 1½"/4 cm. Next Row: Change to larger needles, cont in rib, and inc 1 st at beg and end of row. Cont even in rib until collar measures 3"/7.5 cm from beg. BO in rib.

Placket Edging: With smaller needles and A, pick up and knit 32 sts along right edge of placket, 3 sts from front holder, and 32 sts along left edge of placket—67 sts total. Next Row: BO knitwise.

Sew in zipper. Place markers 8 (9, 9½, 10)"/20.5 (23, 24, 25.5) cm down from shoulders. Set in sleeves between markers. Sew sleeve and side seams.

Child's Fair Isle Patt

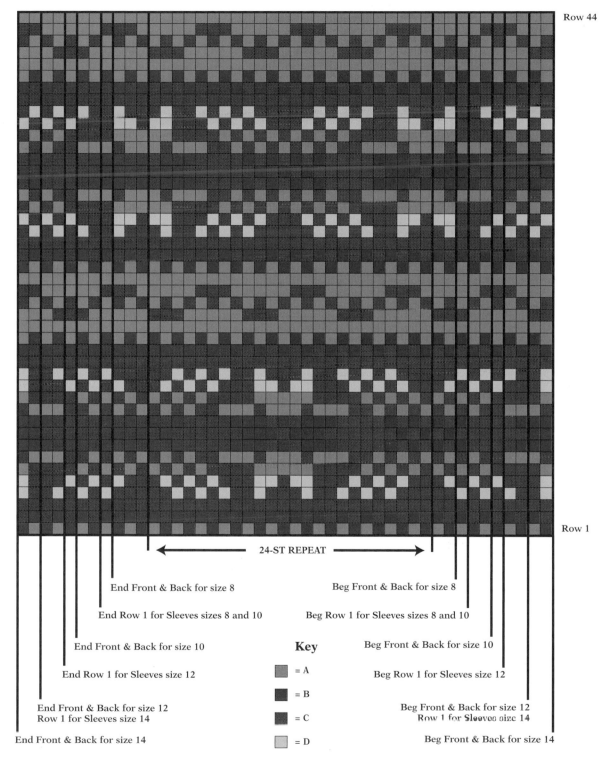

Row 44

Row 1

← 24-ST REPEAT →

End Front & Back for size 8

Beg Front & Back for size 8

End Row 1 for Sleeves sizes 8 and 10

Beg Row 1 for Sleeves sizes 8 and 10

End Front & Back for size 10

Beg Front & Back for size 10

Key

End Row 1 for Sleeves size 12

Beg Row 1 for Sleeves size 12

= A

End Front & Back for size 12
Row 1 for Sleeves size 14

= B

Beg Front & Back for size 12
Row 1 for Sleeves size 14

= C

End Front & Back for size 14

= D

Beg Front & Back for size 14

Toasty
Trio

Occasionally, even accomplished knitters enjoy creating garments that are not the ultimate test of their knitting skills. Here, an easily memorized four-row stitch pattern produces a richly textured, thermal-like fabric with minimal effort.

Woman's Cardigan Vest

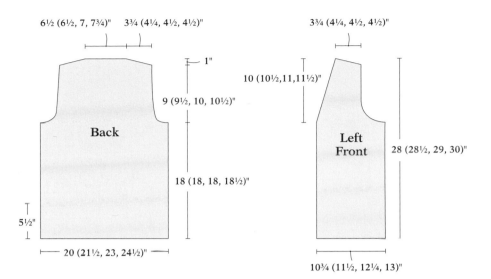

6½ (6½, 7, 7¾)"   3¾ (4¼, 4½, 4½)"   3¾ (4¼, 4½, 4½)"

1"

10 (10½,11,11½)"

9 (9½, 10, 10½)"

Back

Left Front

28 (28½, 29, 30)"

18 (18, 18, 18½)"

5½"

20 (21½, 23, 24½)"

10¾ (11½, 12¼, 13)"

Skill Level
Advanced Beginner

Sizes
Woman's Small (Medium, Large, Extra-Large). Instructions are for smallest size, with changes for other sizes noted in parentheses as necessary.

Finished Measurements
Bust (Buttoned): 40 (43, 46, 49)"/101.5 (109, 117, 124.5) cm
Length: 28 (28½, 29, 30)"/71 (72.5, 73.5, 76) cm

Materials
- Coats/Patons's *Classic Wool* (worsted weight; 100% wool; 3½ oz/100 g; approx 223 yds/204 m), 5 (5, 6, 7) skeins Taupe #227
- Knitting needles, size 7 (4.5 mm) or size needed to obtain gauge
- Two stitch holders
- Five 1"/25 mm buttons (JIID International's *Cherokee* style #98920 was used on sample garment)
- Crochet hook, size G/6 (4.5 mm)

Gauge
In Hurdle Patt, 22 sts and 32 rows = 4"/10 cm. **To save time, take time to check gauge.**

Hurdle Patt (multiple of 2 sts plus 1 st)
Row 1 (RS): Knit.
Row 2: Knit.
Row 3: K1, *P1, K1. Repeat from * across.
Row 4: P1, *K1, P1. Repeat from * across.
Repeat Rows 1–4 for patt.

Back
CO 111 (119, 127, 135) sts. Work even in Hurdle Patt until piece measures 18 (18, 18, 18½)"/45.5 (45.5, 45.5, 47) cm from beg, ending after WS row.
Shape Armholes: BO 4 sts at beg of next four rows, BO 2 sts at beg of next four rows, then dec 1 st each side every other row 5 (6, 5, 5) times, then every row 0 (0, 2, 4) times—77 (83, 89, 93) sts rem. Cont even until armholes measure 9 (9½, 10, 10½)"/23 (24, 25.5, 26.5) cm.
Shape Shoulders: BO 5 (6, 6, 6) sts at beg of next six rows, then BO 6 (6, 7, 7) sts at beg of next two rows. BO rem 35 (35, 39, 43) sts.

Pocket Lining (Make Two)
CO 33 sts. Work Stockinette St for 6½"/16.5 cm, ending after WS row. Slip sts onto holder.

Left Front
CO 59 (63, 67, 71) sts. Work Hurdle Patt until piece measures 7"/18 cm from beg, ending after Row 2 of patt.
Place Pocket Lining: Work across first 8 (10, 12, 14) sts, slip next 33 sts onto holder, cont in Hurdle Patt across 33 sts from one pocket lining, work to end of row. Cont even until piece measures same as back to armhole, ending after WS row.
Shape Armhole and Neck: BO 4 sts at beg of next row. Next Row: Dec 1 st

Designer Hint
Use a loop of contrasting yarn to mark Row 1 of the Hurdle Patt as the RS of the fabric. This way, when seaming, the RS and WS will be easily identifiable.

at beg of row. Cont armhole shaping as for back; **and at the same time,** dec 1 st at neck edge every other row 7 (5, 7, 10) more times, then every fourth row 13 (15, 15, 14) times; **and at the same time,** when piece measures same as back to shoulder, **Shape Shoulder** same as for back.

Place markers for five evenly spaced buttons along front, making the first ½"/1.5 cm from bottom and the last ½"/1.5 cm from beg of neck shaping.

Right Front

Work same as left front, *except* reverse all shaping and pocket placement, and make five 3-st buttonholes opposite markers on RS rows as follows: Work 3 sts in patt, BO next 3 sts, work to end row. On next row, CO 3 sts over the bound-off sts from previous row.

Finishing

Sew shoulder seams.

Pocket Edgings: With RS facing, pick up and knit sts from pocket holder. Work K1 P1 rib for 1"/2.5 cm. BO in rib. Sew pocket linings to WS of fronts. Sew sides of pocket edges to RS of front.

Sew side seams, leaving bottom 5½"/14 cm open for side slits.

Front Edging: With RS facing and crochet hook, attach yarn with a Slip St to lower right front and ch 1. Work one row of sc along right front opening, along back of neck, and down left front opening. End off.

Armhole Edging: With RS facing and crochet hook, attach yarn with a Slip St to underarm and ch 1. Work one rnd of sc along armhole, ending rnd with a Slip St to first sc. End off. Sew on buttons.

Man's Rugby Stripe Pullover

Skill Level
Advanced Beginner

Sizes
Man's Small (Medium, Large, Extra-Large). Instructions are for smallest size, with changes for other sizes noted in parentheses as necessary.

Finished Measurements
Chest: 43 (45, 47, 50)"/109 (114.5, 119.5, 127) cm

Length: 27 (28, 28, 29)"/68.5 (71, 71, 73.5) cm

Sleeve width at upper arm: 20 (20, 21, 22)"/51 (51, 53.5, 56) cm

Materials
- Coats/Patons's *Classic Wool* (worsted weight; 100% wool; 3½ oz/100 g; approx 223 yds/204 m), 7 (7, 8, 9) skeins Dark Natural Mix #228 (**A**) and 1 skein each of Royal Purple #212 (**B**), Taupe #227 (**C**), and Aran #202 (**D**)
- Knitting needles, size 7 (4.5 mm) or size needed to obtain gauge
- 16"/40 cm circular knitting needle, size 6 (4 mm)
- Two stitch holders

Gauge
In Hurdle Patt, 22 sts and 32 rows = 4"/10 cm. **To save time, take time to check gauge.**

Hurdle Patt
Same as for Woman's Cardigan Vest.

Man's Rugby Stripe Pullover

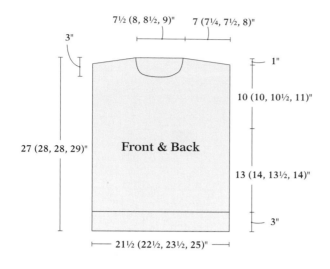

7½ (8, 8½, 9)"　　7 (7¼, 7½, 8)"

3"

1"

10 (10, 10½, 11)"

27 (28, 28, 29)"

Front & Back

13 (14, 13½, 14)"

3"

21½ (22½, 23½, 25)"

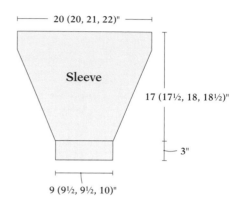

20 (20, 21, 22)"

Sleeve

17 (17½, 18, 18½)"

3"

9 (9½, 9½, 10)"

Back

With A, CO 119 (125, 131, 137) sts. Work K1 P1 rib for 3"/7.5 cm. Next Row (RS): Beg Hurdle Patt. Work even until piece measures 15½ (16½, 15½, 16½)"/39.5 (42, 39.5, 42) cm from beg, ending after Row 4 of patt.

Begin Stripe: Cont in Hurdle Patt and work eight rows each of B, C, D, C, and B. Cont with A until piece measures 26 (27, 27, 28)"/66 (68.5, 68.5, 71) cm from beg.

Shape Shoulders: BO 10 (10, 11, 11) sts at beg of next four rows, then BO 9 (10, 10, 11) sts at beg of next four rows. Slip rem 43 (45, 47, 49) sts onto holder for back of neck.

Front

Work same as back until piece measures 24 (25, 25, 26)"/61 (63.5, 63.5, 66) cm from beg.

Shape Neck: Work across first 51 (54, 56, 59) sts, slip middle 17 (17, 19, 19) sts onto holder for front of neck; join second skein of yarn and work to end row. Work both sides at once with separate skeins of yarn and BO 3 sts each neck edge twice, BO 2 sts each neck edge once (twice, twice, twice), then dec 1 st each neck edge every other row 5 (4, 4, 5) times; **and at the same time,** when front measures same as back to shoulders, **Shape Shoulders** same as for back.

Sleeves

With A, CO 51 (53, 53, 55) st. Work K1 P1 rib for 3"/7.5 cm. Next Row (RS): Beg Hurdle Patt and inc 1 st each side every fourth row 26 (21, 25, 29) times, then every sixth row 4 (8, 6, 4) times— 111 (111, 115, 121) sts. Cont even until sleeve measures 20 (20½, 21, 21½)"/51 (52, 53.5, 54.5) cm from beg. BO.

Finishing

Sew shoulder seams.

Neckband: With RS facing, circular knitting needle, and A, pick up and knit 106 (108, 112, 114) sts. Work rnds of K1 P1 rib for 3"/7.5 cm. BO **loosely** in rib. Fold bound-off edge of band to WS of neckline and **loosely** whipstitch into place.

Place markers 10 (10, 10½, 11)"/25.5 (25.5, 26.5, 28) cm down from shoulders. Set in sleeves between markers. Sew sleeve and side seams.

Child's Cardigan

Skill Level
Intermediate

Sizes
Child's size 2 (4, 6, 8). Instructions are for smallest size, with changes for other sizes noted in parentheses as necessary.

Finished Measurements
Chest (Buttoned): 28 (30, 32, 34)"/71 (76, 81.5, 86.5) cm

Length: 15 (16, 17, 18)"/38 (40.5, 43, 45.5) cm

Sleeve width at upper arm: 13 (14, 15, 16)"/33 (35.5, 38, 40.5) cm

Materials
- Coats/Patons's *Classic Wool* (worsted weight; 100% wool; 3½ oz/100 g; approx 223 yds/204 m), 2 (2, 3, 3) skeins Dark Natural Mix #228 (**A**) and 1 (2, 2, 2) skein each of Taupe #227 (**B**) and Aran #202 (**C**)
- Knitting needles, sizes 6 and 7 (4 and 4.5 mm) or size needed to obtain gauge
- 16"/40 cm circular knitting needle, size 6 (4 mm)
- Two stitch holders
- Two safety pins
- Five (five, six, six) ¾"/20 mm buttons (JHB International's *Helsinki* style #80220 was used on sample garment)

Gauge
With larger needles in Hurdle Patt, 22 sts and 32 rows = 4"/10 cm. **To save time, take time to check gauge.**

Hurdle Patt
Same as for Woman's Cardigan Vest.

Striping Patt
Four rows each of *B, C, A. Repeat from * for patt.

Back
With smaller needles and A, CO 79 (83, 89, 95) sts. Work K1 P1 rib for 1"/2.5 cm. Next Row (RS): Change to larger needles and B, and beg Hurdle Patt. Work even in Hurdle Patt in Striping Patt until piece measures 14¼ (15¼, 16¼, 17¼)"/36 (38.5, 41.5, 44) cm from beg.

Shape Shoulders: BO 8 (8, 9, 10) sts at beg of next four rows, then BO 8 (9, 10, 10) sts at beg of next two rows. BO rem 31 (33, 33, 35) sts.

Pocket Lining (Make Two)
With larger needles and A, CO 15 sts. Work even in Stockinette St for 2½"/6.5 cm, ending after WS row. Slip sts onto holder.

Right Front
With smaller needles and A, CO 44 (46, 50, 52) sts. Work K1 P1 rib for 1"/2.5 cm. Next Row (RS): Rib across first 7 sts and slip them onto safety pin; change to larger needles, join B, and work Hurdle Patt to end row. Cont even in Hurdle Patt in Striping Patt on these 37 (39, 43, 45) sts until piece measures 3½"/9 cm from beg, ending after Row 4 of patt worked in C.

Place Pocket Lining: Change to A and work Row 1 of Hurdle Patt over first 11 (12, 14, 15) sts, slip next 15 sts onto holder; with RS facing, work across 15 sts from one pocket lining holder, work to end of row. Work even until piece measures 10½ (11, 12, 12½)"/26.5 (28, 30.5, 32) cm from beg, ending after WS row.

Child's Cardigan

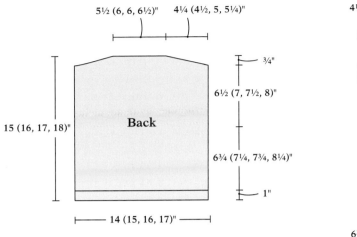

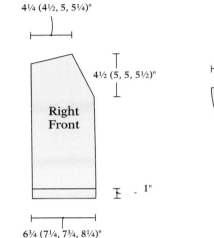

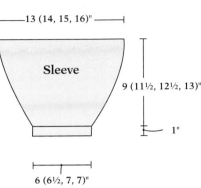

Shape Neck: Dec 1 st at beg of next row. Dec 1 st at neck edge every other row 9 (9, 11, 9) more times, then every fourth row 3 (4, 3, 5) times; **and at the same time,** when piece measures same as back to shoulder, **Shape Shoulder** same as for back.

Left Front

Work same as right front until piece measures ½"/1.5 cm from beg. Next Row (WS): Work in rib as established across first 2 sts, BO next 2 sts, work to end row. Next Row: Work rib as established, CO 2 sts over the bound-off sts from previous row. Work even in rib as established until piece measures 1"/2.5 cm from beg, ending after WS row. Next Row (RS): Change to larger needles and B, and work Hurdle Patt until 7 sts rem in row. Slip these 7 sts onto safety pin. Complete same as right front, *except* reverse all shaping and pocket placement.

Sleeves

With smaller needles and A, CO 33 (35, 39, 39) sts. Work K1 P1 rib for 1"/2.5 cm. Next Row (RS): Change to larger needles and B, beg Hurdle Patt in Striping Patt, and inc 1 st each side every other row 8 (0, 0, 2) times, then every fourth row 12 (21, 20, 23) times, then every sixth row 0 (0, 2, 0) times—73 (77, 83, 89) sts. Work even until sleeve measures 10 (12½, 13½, 14)"/25.5 (32, 34.5, 35.5) cm from beg. BO.

Finishing

Sew shoulder seams.

Button Band: With smaller needles and A, pick up the 7 sts from safety pin on right front, and work K1 P1 rib until band when slightly stretched fits along front edge to center of back. BO. Neatly sew into place along edge of front. Place markers for four (four, five, five) more evenly spaced buttons along band, making the first ½"/1.5 cm below start of neck shaping.

Buttonhole Band: With smaller needles and A, pick up sts from safety pin on left front and work same as button band, *except* make 2-st buttonholes opposite markers, keeping in mind that band will be slightly stretched when sewn onto front. Sew bound-off edges of bands tog at back of neck.

Pocket Edges: With smaller needles and A, pick up and knit sts from pocket holder. Work K1 P1 rib for ¾"/2 cm. BO in rib. Sew pocket linings to WS of fronts. Sew sides of pocket edges to RS of front.
Place markers 6½ (7, 7½, 8)"/16.5 (18, 19, 20.5) cm down from shoulders. Set in sleeves between markers. Sew sleeve and side seams. Sew on buttons.

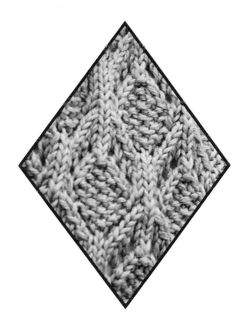

Pastoral Pastels

An exquisite textured lace pattern graces these

delicate pastel knits. Special details include

an empire waist on the dainty Girl's Dress and

a button closure on the Baby's All-in-One

for fast and easy changes. Bobbles add a bit

of whimsy, and the soft cotton/wool yarn

adds a touch of luxury.

Woman's Cropped Cardigan

Skill Level
Intermediate

Sizes
Woman's Small (Medium, Large, Extra-Large). Instructions are for smallest size, with changes for other sizes noted in parentheses as necessary.

Finished Measurements
Bust (Buttoned): 37 (40, 44, 47½)"/94 (101.5, 112, 120.5) cm
Length: 18 (18½, 19, 20)"/46 (47, 48, 51) cm
Sleeve width at upper arm: 16 (17, 17, 18)"/40.5 (43, 43, 45.5) cm

Materials
• Brown Sheep Company's *Cotton Fleece* (light worsted weight; 80% pima cotton/20% merino wool; 3½ oz/100 m; approx 215 yds/197 m), 6 (7, 7, 8) skeins Alpine Lilac #CW-690
• Knitting needles, sizes 4 and 6 (3.5 and 4 mm) or size needed to obtain gauge
• Six (six, seven, seven) ¾"/20 mm buttons (JHB International's *Silver Sheen* style #70796 was used on sample garment)

Gauge
With larger needles in Lace Patt, 22 sts and 30 rows = 4"/10 cm. **To save time, take time to check gauge.**

Bobble
(K1, yarn over) twice into next st, K1 again into same st, turn; P5, turn; K5, turn; p2tog, P1, p2tog, turn; slip 2 sts knitwise, K1, p2sso.

Designer Hint

For perky bobbles, choose one of the following techniques: On the WS row after the bobble, either (1) slip each bobble stitch purlwise with the yarn tightly in front or (2) knit into the back loop of the bobble stitch to twist it.

Back

With smaller needles, CO 101 (111, 121, 131) sts. Work four rows Garter St. Next Row (RS): K5, *Bobble, K4. Repeat from * across, ending row with Bobble, K5. Work four more rows of Garter St. Next Row (WS): Change to larger needles, and purl across. Beg and end where indicated, work Lace Patt until piece measures 10 (10, 10½, 11)"/25.5 (25.5, 26.5, 28) cm from beg.

Shape Armholes: BO 10 sts at beg of next two rows—81 (91, 101, 111) sts rem. Cont even until armholes measure 8 (8½, 8½, 9)"/20.5 (21.5, 21.5, 23) cm. BO.

Right Front

With smaller needles, CO 51 (55, 61, 65) sts. Work four rows Garter St. Next Row (RS): K5 (2, 5, 2), *Bobble, K4. Repeat from * across, ending row with Bobble, K5 (2, 5, 2). Work four more rows of Garter St. Next Row (WS): Change to larger needles and purl across. Beg and end where indicated, work Lace Patt until piece measures 10 (10, 10½, 11)"/25.5 (25.5, 26.5, 28) cm from beg, ending after RS row.

Shape Armhole: BO 10 sts at beg of next row. Cont even until armhole measures 5½ (6, 6, 6½)"/14 (15, 15, 16.5) cm, ending after WS row.

Shape Neck: BO 5 sts at neck edge once, BO 3 sts at neck edge once, BO 2 sts at neck edge 2 (2, 3, 3) times, then dec 1 st at neck edge every other row three times—26 (30, 34, 38) sts rem. Cont even until piece measures same as back to shoulders. BO.

Left Front

Work same as right front, *except* reverse all shaping.

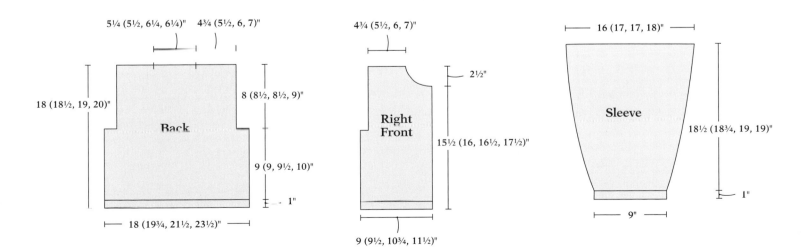

Lace Patt

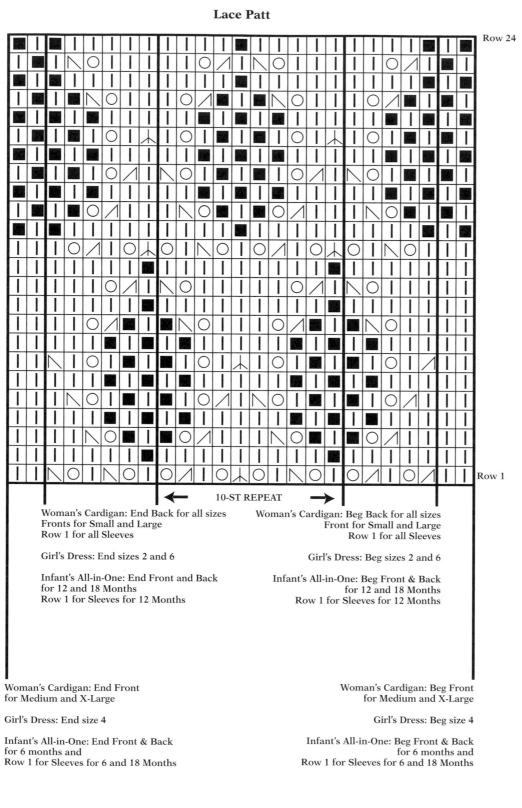

Row 24

Row 1

← **10-ST REPEAT** →

Woman's Cardigan: End Back for all sizes
Fronts for Small and Large
Row 1 for all Sleeves

Girl's Dress: End sizes 2 and 6

Infant's All-in-One: End Front and Back
for 12 and 18 Months
Row 1 for Sleeves for 12 Months

Woman's Cardigan: Beg Back for all sizes
Front for Small and Large
Row 1 for all Sleeves

Girl's Dress: Beg sizes 2 and 6

Infant's All-in-One: Beg Front & Back
for 12 and 18 Months
Row 1 for Sleeves for 12 Months

Woman's Cardigan: End Front
for Medium and X-Large

Girl's Dress: End size 4

Infant's All-in-One: End Front & Back
for 6 months and
Row 1 for Sleeves for 6 and 18 Months

Woman's Cardigan: Beg Front
for Medium and X-Large

Girl's Dress: Beg size 4

Infant's All-in-One: Beg Front & Back
for 6 months and
Row 1 for Sleeves for 6 and 18 Months

Key

	= Knit on RS; purl on WS
■	= Purl on RS; knit on WS
○	= Yarn over
⟋	= K2tog
⟍	= Ssk
⋀	= Slip 2 sts; K1; p2sso

Sleeves

With smaller needles, CO 51 sts. Work four rows Garter St. Next Row (RS): K5, Bobble, K4. Repeat from * across, ending row with Bobble, K5. Work four more rows of Garter St. Next Row (WS): Change to larger needles and purl across. Beg and end where indicated, work Lace Patt, and inc 1 st each side every fourth row 0 (2, 2, 12) times, then every sixth row 19 (19, 19, 12) times—89 (93, 93, 99) sts. Cont even until sleeve measures 19½ (19¾, 20, 20)"/49.5 (50, 51, 51) cm from beg. BO.

Finishing

Sew shoulder seams.

Button Band: With RS facing and smaller needles, pick up and K87 (90, 93, 99) evenly along left front edge. Work Garter St for 1"/2.5 cm. BO. Place markers for six (six, seven, seven) evenly spaced buttons along band, making the first ½"/1.5 cm from bottom and the last ½"/1.5 cm from beg of neck shaping.

Buttonhole Band: Work same as button band until band measures ½"/1.5 cm. Next Row: BO 3 sts opposite markers. Next Row: Knit, CO 3 sts over the bound-off sts from previous row. Complete as for button band.

Collar: With RS facing and smaller needles, pick up and K71 (71, 76, 76) evenly along neck edge, beg and end at center of front bands. Work Garter St for 2"/5 cm. Change to larger needles, and cont in Garter St until collar measures 2½"/6.5 cm, ending after RS row. Next Row: K5, *Bobble, K4. Repeat from * across, ending row with Bobble, K5. Work four more rows of Garter St. BO.

Set in sleeves. Sew sleeve and side seams. Sew on buttons.

Girl's Dress

Skill Level
Intermediate

Sizes
Child's size 2 (4, 6). Instructions are for smallest size, with changes for other sizes noted in parentheses as necessary.

Finished Measurements
Chest: 22 (24, 26)"/56 (61, 66) cm
Length: 19 (20, 21)"/48.5 (51, 53.5) cm
Sleeve width at upper arm: 10 (10½, 11)"/25.5 (26.5, 28) cm

Materials
- Brown Sheep Company's *Cotton Fleece* (light worsted weight; 80% pima cotton/20% merino wool; 3½ oz/100 m; approx 215 yds/197 m), 4 (4, 5) skeins Victorian Pink #CW-230
- Knitting needles, sizes 4 and 6 (3.5 and 4 mm) or size needed to obtain gauge
- Four ½"/15 mm buttons (JHB International's *Anaheim* style #44831 in Pink was used on sample garment)
- Two stitch holders

Gauge
With larger needles in Stockinette St, 21 sts and 28 rows = 4"/10 cm.
With larger needles in Lace Patt, 22 sts and 30 rows = 4"/10 cm. **To save time, take time to check gauge.**

Bobble
Same as for Woman's Cropped Cardigan.

Back

With smaller needles, CO 85 (91, 95) sts. Work four rows Garter St. Next Row (RS): K2 (5, 2), *Bobble, K4. Repeat from * across, ending row with Bobble, K2 (5, 2). Work four more rows of Garter St. Next Row (WS): Change to larger needles, and purl across. Work Stockinette St until piece measures 12½ (13½, 14½)"/32 (34.5, 37) cm from beg, ending after WS row. Next Row (RS): Change to smaller needles, and knit across, dec 24 (25, 24) sts evenly across—61 (66, 71) sts rem. Work three rows Garter St. Next Row (RS): K5, *Bobble, K4. Repeat from * across, ending row with Bobble, K5. Work four more rows of Garter St, dec 0 (1, 0) sts at end of last row—61 (65, 71) sts. Next Row (WS): Change to larger needles, and purl across. Beg and end where indicated, work Lace Patt until piece measures 14½ (15, 15½)"/37 (38, 39.5) cm from beg.

Shape Armholes: BO 4 sts at beg of next two rows, then dec 1 st each side every other row 4 (3, 4) times—45 (51, 55) sts rem. Cont even until armholes measure 4½ (5, 5½)"/11.5 (12.5, 14) cm, ending after WS row. Next Row (RS): BO first 36 (39, 41) sts, slip rem 9 (12, 14) sts onto holder for left shoulder.

Front

Work same as for back until armholes measure 1½ (2, 2½)"/4 (5, 6.5) cm.

Shape Neck: Work across first 16 (19, 21) sts; join second skein of yarn and BO middle 13 sts, work to end row. Work both sides at once with separate skeins of yarn, and BO 2 sts each neck edge twice, then dec 1 st each neck edge every other row three times. Cont even until armhole measures 3½ (4, 4½)"/9 (10, 11.5) cm, ending after WS

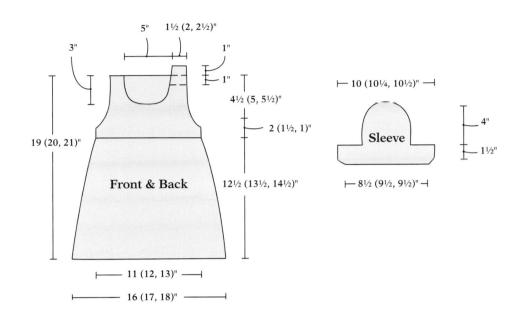

5"   1½ (2, 2½)"
3"
1"
1"
4½ (5, 5½)"
2 (1½, 1)"
19 (20, 21)"
Front & Back
12½ (13½, 14½)"
11 (12, 13)"
16 (17, 18)"

10 (10¼, 10½)"
Sleeve
4"
1½"
8½ (9½, 9½)"

row. Slip 9 (12, 14) sts onto holder for left shoulder. Cont even on right shoulder until right armhole measures 4½ (5, 5½)"/11.5 (12.5, 14) cm. BO.

Sleeves

With smaller needles, CO 46 (51, 51) sts. Work four rows Garter St. Next Row (RS): K5, *Bobble, K4. Repeat from * across, ending row with Bobble, K5. Work four more rows of Garter St. Next Row (WS): Change to larger needles, beg Stockinette St, and inc 1 st each side every row 4 (2, 3) times—54 (55, 57) sts. Cont even until sleeve measures 1½"/4 cm from the beg.

Shape Cap: BO 4 sts at beg of next two rows. Dec 1 st each side every other row eleven times. BO 3 sts at beg of next four rows; then BO rem 12 (13, 15) sts.

Finishing

Sew right shoulder seam.

Neckband: With RS facing and smaller needles, pick up and K85 around neckline. Work three rows Garter St. Next Row (RS): K2, *Bobble, K4. Repeat from * across, ending row with Bobble, K2. Work three more rows of Garter St, dec 7 sts evenly across first row—78 sts. BO.

Button Band: With smaller needles, pick up and K7 along side of neckband, then K9 (12, 14) from back left shoulder holder—16 (19, 21) sts total. Work Garter St for 1"/2.5 cm. BO. Place markers for four evenly spaced buttons along band.

Buttonhole Band: Work same as button band along front left shoulder until band measures ½"/1.5 cm. Make four buttonholes opposite markers by working (k2tog, yarn over). Complete same as for button band.

Overlap buttonhole band over button band, and sew armhole ends tog. Set in sleeves. Sew sleeve and side seams. Sew on buttons.

Baby's All-in-One

Skill level

Intermediate

Sizes

Infant's size 6 (12, 18) months. Instructions are for smallest size, with changes for other sizes noted in parentheses as necessary.

Finished Measurements

Chest: 26 (28, 30)"/66 (71, 76) cm
Length: 21 (22½, 24)"/53.5 (57, 61) cm
Sleeve width at upper arm: 11 (12, 13)"/28 (30.5, 33) cm

Materials

- Brown Sheep Company's *Cotton Fine* (fingering weight; 80% pima cotton/20% merino wool, ½ lb/226 g, approx 1000 yds/910 m), 2 (2, 2) cones Banana #CF-620
- Knitting needles, sizes 0 and 2 (2 and 2.5 mm) or size needed to obtain gauge
- Thirteen ⅜"/10 mm buttons (JHB International's *Classic Pearl* style #70160 was used on sample garment)
- Two stitch holders

Gauge

With larger needles in Stockinette St, 32 sts and 42 rows = 4"/10 cm.
With larger needles in Lace Patt, 32 sts and 48 rows = 4"/10 cm. **To save time, take time to check gauge.**

Bobble

Same as for Woman's Cropped Cardigan.

Back

Left Leg: With smaller needles, CO 31 (41, 51) sts. Work four rows Garter St. Next Row (RS): K5, *Bobble, K4. Repeat from * across, ending row with Bobble, K5. Work four more rows of Garter St. Next Row (WS): Change to larger needles, and purl across. Cont in Stockinette St, and inc 1 st each side every fourth row 11 (5, 1) times, then every sixth row 2 (2, 0) times, then every tenth row 0 (3, 6) times—57 (61, 65) sts. Cont even until leg measures 6½ (7, 7½)"/16.5 (18, 19) cm from beg, ending after WS row.

Shape Crotch: BO 2 sts at beg of next row, then dec 1 st this side each row 2 (3, 2) times. Slip rem 53 (56, 61) sts onto holder.

Right Leg: Work same as for left leg, *except* reverse shaping.

Join Legs: Knit across 53 (56, 61) sts from right leg and 53 (56, 61) sts from left leg—106 (112, 122) sts. Work even in Stockinette St until piece measures 12½ (13½, 14½)"/32 (34.5, 37) cm from beg, ending after WS row. Change to smaller needles, and work four rows Garter St, dec 1 st at beg of first row—105 (111, 121) sts rem. Next Row (RS):K2 (5, 5), Bobble, K4. Repeat from * across, ending row with Bobble, K2 (5, 5). Work four more rows of Garter St. Next Row (WS): Change to larger needles, and purl across. Beg and end where indicated, work Lace Patt until piece measures 15½ (16½, 17½)"/39.5 (42, 44.5) cm from beg.

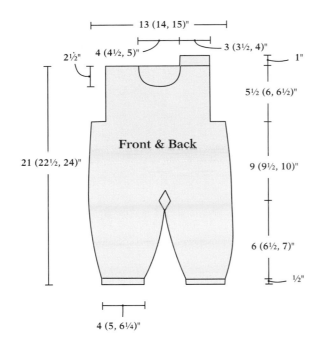

13 (14, 15)"

4 (4½, 5)"

2½"

3 (3½, 4)"

1"

5½ (6, 6½)"

Front & Back

21 (22½, 24)"

9 (9½, 10)"

6 (6½, 7)"

½"

4 (5, 6¼)"

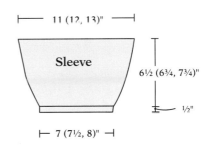

11 (12, 13)"

Sleeve

6½ (6¾, 7¾)"

½"

7 (7½, 8)"

Shape Armholes: BO 12 (10, 10) sts at beg of next two rows—81 (91, 101) sts rem. Cont even until armholes measure 5½ (6, 6½)"/14 (15, 16.5) cm, ending after WS row. BO first 56 (63, 70) sts, knit to end row. Slip rem 25 (28, 31) sts onto holder for left shoulder.

Front

Work same as back until armholes measure 3 (3½, 4)"/7.5 (9, 10) cm from the beg.

Shape Neck: Work across first 34 (38, 42) sts; join second cone of yarn and BO middle 13 (15, 17) sts, work to end row. Work both sides at once and BO 3 sts each neck edge once, BO 2 sts each neck edge twice, then dec 1 st each neck edge every other row 2 (3, 4) times. Cont even until armhole measures 4½ (5, 5½)"/11.5 (12.5, 14) cm, ending after WS row. Slip 25 (28, 31) sts onto holder for left shoulder. Cont even on right shoulder until right armhole measures 5½ (6, 6½)"/ 14 (15, 16.5) cm. BO.

Sleeves

With smaller needles, CO 55 (61, 65) sts. Work four rows Garter St. Next Row (RS): K2 (5, 2), *Bobble, K4. Repeat from * across, ending row with Bobble, K2 (5, 2). Work four more rows of Garter St. Next Row (WS): Change to larger needles, and purl across. Beg and end where indicated, work Lace Patt and inc 1 st each side every other row 8 (8, 7) times, then every fourth row 9 (10, 13) times—89 (97, 105) sts. Cont even until piece measures 7 (7¼, 8¼)"/18 (18.5, 21) cm from beg. BO.

Finishing

Sew right shoulder seam.

Inseam Bands: With smaller needles, CO 10 sts. Work Garter St for 12½ (13½, 14½)"/32 (34.5, 37) cm. BO. Place markers for nine evenly spaced buttons along band, making the first and last ½"/1.5 cm from the edges. Make a second band, making nine 2-st buttonholes opposite markers on first band. On row after buttonholes, CO

2 sts over the bound-off sts from previous row. Sew on inseam bands with the buttonhole band on the front.

Neckband: With RS facing and smaller needles, pick up and K85 (90, 95) around neckline. Work four rows Garter St. Next Row (RS): K2, *Bobble, K4. Repeat from * across, ending row with Bobble, K2. Work four more rows of Garter St. BO.

Button Band: With smaller needles, pick up and K5 along side of neckband, then K25 (28, 31) from back left shoulder—30 (33, 36) sts total. Work Garter St for 1"/2.5 cm. BO. Place markers for four evenly spaced buttons along band.

Buttonhole Band: Work same as button band along front left shoulder until band measures ½"/1.5 cm. Next Row: Knit, and make four 2-st buttonholes opposite markers. Next Row: CO 2 sts over the bound-off sts from previous row. Complete same as for button band.

Overlap buttonhole band over button band and sew armhole ends tog. Set in sleeves. Sew sleeve and side seams. Sew on buttons.

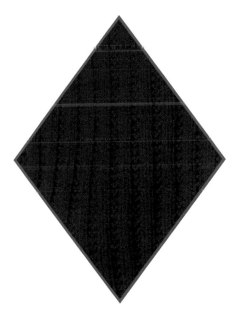

Riot
of Ribs

*Fully fashioned shaping comes to the forefront in
this his and hers raglan duo. In the man's sweater,
diverging ribs form an integrated V-neckline.
Likewise, the woman's mock turtleneck flows
seamlessly from the already established rib pattern.
Both projects are wonderful to create, combining
simple knitting with interesting shaping techniques.*

Woman's Mock Turtleneck Pullover

Skill Level
Intermediate

Sizes
Woman's Small (Medium, Large, Extra-Large). Instructions are for smallest size, with changes for other sizes noted in parentheses as necessary.

Finished Measurements
Bust: 37 (40, 43, 46)"/94 (101.5, 109, 117) cm
Length: 19½ (20, 21, 22)"/49.5 (51, 53.5, 56) cm
Sleeve width at upper arm: 14 (14, 15½, 15½)"/35.5 (35.5, 39.5, 39.5) cm

Materials
- Lane Borgosesia/Baruffa's *Maratona®* (light worsted weight; 100% wool; 1¾ oz/50 g; approx 121 yds/110 m), 11 (12, 13, 14) balls Mulberry #60255
- Knitting needles, size 7 (4.5 mm) or size needed to obtain gauge
- 16"/40 cm circular knitting needle, size 7 (4.5 mm)
- Four stitch holders

Gauge
In Garter Rib Patt, 22 sts and 36 rows = 4"/10 cm. **To save time, take time to check gauge.**

Garter Rib Patt (multiple of 4 sts plus 2 sts)
Row 1 (RS): K2, *P2, K2 through back loop. Repeat from * across.
Row 2: Purl.
Repeat Rows 1 and 2 for patt.

Designer Hint

When working these raglan decreases, place markers between the 5th and 6th sts in from both sides. Make your Fully Fashioned Decreases just inside these markers as follows: work to first marker, ssk; work across row to 2 sts before next marker, k2tog, work to end of row.

Fully Fashioned Decreases

Work fully fashioned decreases on RS rows as follows: K2, P2, K1, ssk. Work in patt as established until 7 sts rem, k2tog, K1, P2, K2.

Back

CO 102 (110, 118, 126) sts. Work Garter Rib Patt until piece measures 10½ (10½, 11, 11½)"/26.5 (26.5, 28, 29) cm from beg.

Shape Raglan: BO 4 sts at beg of next two rows, then work Fully Fashioned Decreases every fourth row 4 (2, 4, 3) times, then every other row 28 (34, 32, 37) times. Slip rem 30 (30, 38, 38) sts onto holder for back of neck.

Front

Work same as for back.

Sleeves

CO 46 (46, 54, 54) sts. Work Garter Rib Patt and inc 1 st each side every eighth row 10 (10, 8, 6) times, then every tenth row 6 (6, 8, 10) times—78 (78, 86, 86) sts. Work even until sleeve measures 17 (17, 17½, 18)"/43 (43, 44.5, 45.5) cm from beg.

Shape Raglan: BO 4 sts at beg of next two rows, then work Fully Fashioned Decreases every fourth row 6 (8, 6, 9) times, then every other row 23 (21, 27, 24) times. Work one row even on rem

12 sts. Next Row (RS): K2, P2, ssk, k2tog, P2, K2. Slip these 10 sts onto holder.

Finishing

Sew raglan seams.

Neckband: With circular knitting needle, beg with one sleeve and work *k2tog, cont in Garter Rib Patt for 6 sts, ssk, k2tog, cont in Garter Rib Patt for 26 (26, 34, 34) sts, ssk. Repeat from * once more. Cont in rnds of Garter Rib Patt on these 72 (72, 88, 88) sts for 5"/12.5 cm as follows: Rnd 1: K2, P2; repeat from * around. Rnd 2: Knit. Repeat Rnds 1 and 2 for patt. BO **loosely.** Fold neckband in half and **loosely** whipstitch into place. Sew sleeve and side seams.

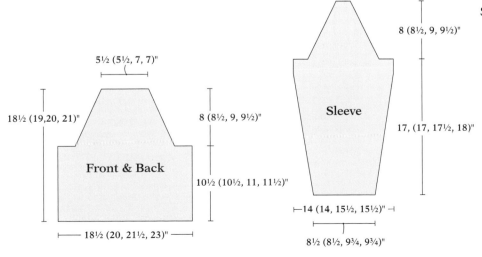

Man's V-Neck Pullover

Skill Level
Intermediate

Sizes
Man's Small (Medium, Large, Extra-Large). Instructions are for smallest size, with changes for other sizes noted in parentheses as necessary.

Finished Measurements
Chest: 42½ (45, 48½, 51)"/108 (114.5, 123, 129.5) cm

Length: 25 (26, 26, 27)"/63.5 (66, 66, 68.5) cm

Sleeve width at upper arm: 16 (17, 17, 18)"/40.5 (43, 43, 45.5) cm

Materials
* Lane Borgosesia/Baruffa's *Maratona*® (light worsted weight; 100% wool; 1¾ oz/50 g; approx 121 yds/110 m), 16 (16, 17, 18) balls Lapis #638
* Knitting needles, size 7 (4.5 mm) or size needed to obtain gauge
* Cable needle
* Two stitch holders

Gauge
In Garter Rib Patt, 22 sts and 36 rows = 4"/10 cm. **To save time, take time to check gauge.**

Garter Rib Patt
Same as for Woman's Mock Turtleneck Pullover.

Fully Fashioned Decreases
Same as for Woman's Mock Turtleneck Pullover.

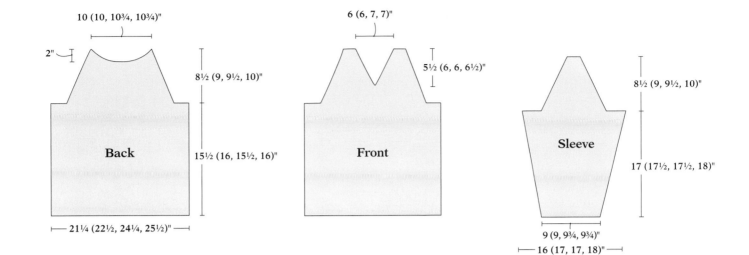

Back

CO 118 (126, 134, 142) sts. Work Garter Rib Patt until piece measures 15½ (16, 15½, 16)"/39.5 (40.5, 39.5, 40.5) cm from beg.

Shape Raglan: BO 4 sts at beg of next two rows, then work Fully Fashioned Decreases every fourth row 11 (9, 9, 8) times, then every other row 16 (22, 24, 29) times; **and at the same time,** when armholes measure 6½ (7, 7½, 8)"/16.5 (18, 19, 20.5) cm, shape neck by binding off middle 38 (38, 42, 42) sts and then work Fully Fashioned Decrease each neck edge every other row nine times.

Front

Work same as back until piece measures 15½ (16, 15½, 16)"/39.5 (40.5, 39.5, 40.5) cm from beg.

Shape Raglan and Neck: BO 4 sts at beg of next two rows, then work Fully Fashioned Decreases every fourth row 7 (7, 8, 8) times—96 (104, 110, 118) sts rem. Cont shaping armholes same as for back, and on next RS row, work across first 36 (40, 43, 47) sts, k2tog, K1, (P2, K2) twice, P1, join second ball of yarn and work P1, (K2, P2) twice, K1, ssk, cont in rib as established to end row. Work neck decreases every other row 9 (7, 11, 8) more times, then every fourth row 7 (9, 7, 10) times; **and at the same time,** work Fully Fashioned Decreases same as for back—11 sts rem each side. Slip these sts onto holders.

Sleeves

CO 50 (50, 54, 54) sts. Work Garter Rib Patt and inc 1 st each side every sixth row 10 (16, 8, 14) times, then every eighth row 10 (6, 12, 8) times—90 (94, 94, 98) sts. Work even until sleeve measures 17 (17½, 17½, 18)"/43 (44.5, 44.5, 45.5) cm from beg.

Shape Raglan: BO 4 sts at beg of next two rows, then work Fully Fashioned Decreases every fourth row 2 (2, 4, 5) times, then every other row 33 (35, 33, 34) times. Work one row even on rem 12 sts. Next Row (RS): K2, P2, ssk, k2tog, P2, K2. BO these 10 rem sts.

Finishing

Sew raglan seams.

Neckband: Pick up the 11 sts from one stitch holder, and inc 1 st for seaming on shoulder edge—12 sts. Cont in Garter Rib Patt until the band, when slightly stretched, fits to center back of neck. Repeat for second side. Graft the center back of neckband tog. Sew band into place. Sew sleeve and side seams.

Bird's-Eye Bulkies

Here's one of those great stitch patterns that looks more complicated than it really is. Crossed slip stitches create a textured bird's-eye tweed while using only one color per row. With thick yarn and large needles, these projects will knit up quickly.

Woman's Cardigan

Skill Level
Intermediate

Sizes
Woman's Small (Medium, Large).
Instructions are for the smallest size,
with changes for larger sizes noted in
parentheses as necessary.

Finished Measurements
Bust (Buttoned): 37½ (40½, 46½)"/95
   (102.5, 118) cm
Length: 20 (21, 22)"/51 (53.5, 56) cm
Sleeve width at upper arm: 18 (19,
   20)"/45.5 (48.5, 51) cm

Materials
* JCA/Reynolds's *Lopi* (bulky weight;
  100% wool, 3½ oz/100 g; approx 110
  yds/100 m), 6 (6, 7) skeins Marigold
  #72 (**A**); 3 (3, 4) skeins Hyacinth
  Violet #390 (**B**); and 2 (2, 3) skeins
  Jade Heather #28 (**C**)
* Knitting needles, sizes 9 and 10½
  (5.5 and 6.5 mm) or size needed to
  obtain gauge
* Six ⅞"/20 mm buttons (JHB
  International's *Abstract* style #36005
  in Purple and White was used on
  sample garment)
* Two safety pins
* Three stitch holders

Gauge
With larger needles in Bird's-Eye Slip
St Patt, 16 sts and 24 rows = 4"/10 cm.
**To save time, take time to check
gauge.**

RT (Right Twist)
K2tog without slipping them off LH
needle; insert RH needle between the
same 2 sts and knit the first one again;
slip them both off LH needle.

Designer Hint

The instructions for these sweaters include one selvage Stockinette St on each side to aid in seaming the garment. Always work your increases and decreases inside these stitches for neater finishing.

LT (Left Twist)

Skip 1 st; knit next st through back loop; then knit the skipped st in front loop; slip them both off LH needle.

Color Sequence

*2 rows each of B, A, C, A. Repeat from * for patt.

Bird's-Eye Slip St Patt (multiple of 6 sts)

Row 1 (RS): K5, *slip next 2 sts with yarn in back, K4. Repeat from * across, ending row with slip next 2 sts with yarn in back, K5.

Row 2: P5, *slip next 2 sts with yarn in front, P4. Repeat from * across, ending row with slip next 2 sts with yarn in front, P5.

Row 3: K2, *slip next 2 sts with yarn in back, RT, LT. Repeat from * across, ending row with slip next 2 sts with yarn in back, K2.

Row 4: Purl.

Row 5: K2, *slip next 2 sts with yarn in back, K4. Repeat from * across, ending row with slip next 2 sts with yarn in back, K2.

Row 6: P2, *slip next 2 sts with yarn in front, P4. Repeat from * across, ending row with slip next 2 sts with yarn in front, P2.

Row 7: K1, *RT, LT, slip next 2 sts with yarn in back. Repeat from * across, ending row with RT, LT, K1.

Row 8: Purl.

Repeat Rows 1–8 in Color Sequence for patt.

Back

With smaller needles and B, CO 72 (84, 96) sts. Change to A, and work K1 P1 rib until piece measures 1½"/4 cm from beg. Next Row (WS): Purl across. Change to larger needles and B, and work Bird's-Eye Slip St Patt in Color Sequence until piece measures 10 (10½, 11)"/25.5 (26.5, 28) cm from beg.

Shape Armholes: BO 9 (9, 15) sts at beg of next two rows—54 (66, 66) sts rem. Cont even until armholes measure 9 (9½, 10)"/23 (24, 25.5) cm.

Shape Shoulders: BO 3 (5, 5) sts at beg of next six rows, then BO 4 sts at beg of next two rows. Slip rem 28 sts onto holder for back of neck.

Left Front

With smaller needles and B, CO 43 (43, 49) sts. Change to A, and work K1 P1 rib until piece measures 1½"/4 cm from beg. Next Row (WS): Work rib as established across first 7 sts and place them onto safety pin, purl across rem 36 (36, 42) sts to end row. Change to larger needles and B, and work Bird's-Eye Slip St Patt in Color Sequence until piece measures 10 (10½, 11)"/25.5 (26.5, 28) cm from beg, ending after WS row.

Shape Armhole: BO 9 (9, 15) sts at beg of next row—27 sts rem. Cont even until piece measures 17 (18, 19)"/43 (45.5, 48.5) cm from beg, ending after RS row.

Shape Neck: BO 3 sts at neck edge 1 (0, 0) time, then BO 2 sts at neck edge 3 (2, 2) times, then dec 1 st at neck edge every other row 5 (4, 4) times; **and at the same time,** when piece measures same as back to shoulders, **Shape Shoulders** same as for back.

Right Front

Work same as for left front, *except* reverse all shaping and work one buttonhole on ribbed band when piece

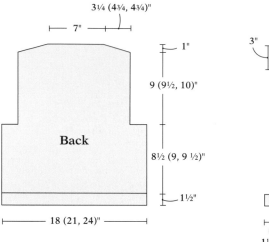

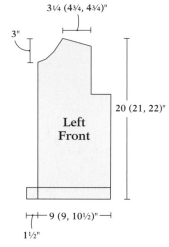

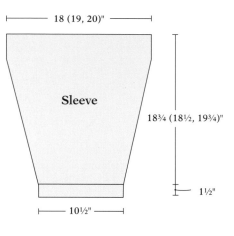

measures ½"/1.5 cm from beg by working (K1, P1, BO next 3 sts, P1, K1) at beg of a RS row. Next Row: CO 3 sts over the bound-off sts of previous row. When piece measures 1½"/4 cm from beg, slip these 7 sts onto safety pin as before.

Sleeves
With smaller needles and B, CO 42 sts. Change to A, and work K1 P1 rib until piece measures 1½"/4 cm from beg. Next Row (WS): Change to larger needles and B, and work Bird's-Eye Slip St Patt in Color Sequence and inc 1 st each side every fourth row 0 (0, 7) times, inc 1 st each side every sixth row 8 (17, 12) times, then inc 1 st each side every eighth row 7 (0, 0) times—

72 (76, 80) sts. Cont even until sleeve measures 20¼ (20, 21¼)"/51.5 (51, 54) cm from beg. BO.

Finishing
Sew shoulder seams.

Button Band: With smaller needles and A, pick up sts from safety pin on left front, and work K1 P1 rib until band, when slightly stretched, fits along front. Slip sts to safety pin again, and neatly sew into place along edge of front. Place markers for five evenly spaced buttons along band, making the first ½"/1.5 cm from bottom and the last 3 (3, 3¼)"/7.5 (7.5, 8.5) cm from top.

Buttonhole Band: With smaller needles and A, pick up sts from safety pin on right front, and work same as button band, *except* make 3-st

buttonholes opposite markers, keeping in mind that band will be slightly stretched when sewn onto front. Slip these sts to safety pin again, and neatly sew band into place along edge of front.

Neckband: With RS facing, smaller needles, and A, keeping first and last 7 sts from safety pins in rib as established, pick up and K68 around neckline, including sts from neck holder and safety pins. Work K1 P1 rib for ½"/1.5 cm. Make buttonhole on right front edge as before. Cont in rib until neckband measures 1"/2.5 cm from beg. Change to B, work one row in rib, then BO in rib.

Set in sleeves. Sew sleeve and side seams. Sew on buttons.

Man's Cardigan

Skill Level
Intermediate

Sizes
Man's Small (Medium, Large, Extra-Large). Instructions are for smallest size, with changes for other sizes noted in parentheses as necessary.

Finished Measurements
Chest (Buttoned): 43 (44½, 49, 50½)"/109 (113, 124.5, 128.5) cm
Length: 28 (29, 29, 30)"/71 (73.5, 73.5, 76) cm
Sleeve width at upper arm: 19 (20, 21, 22)"/48.5 (51, 53.5, 56) cm

Materials
- JCA/Reynolds's *Lopi* (bulky weight; 100% wool, 3½ oz/100 g; approx 110 yds/100 m), 7 (8, 9, 10) skeins Copper #384 (**A**); 4 (4, 4, 5) skeins Adirondack Green #172 (**B**); and 3 (3, 3, 4) skeins Persimmon #171 (**C**)
- Knitting needles, sizes 9 and 10½ (5.5 and 6.5 mm) or size needed to obtain gauge
- 29"/80 cm circular knitting needle, size 9 (5.5 mm)
- Three stitch holders
- Six ⅞"/22 mm buttons (JHB International's *Surrey* style #62110 Fawn Brown was used on sample garment)
- Crochet hook, size I/9 (5.5 mm)

Gauge
With larger needles in Bird's-Eye Slip St Patt, 16 sts and 24 rows = 4"/10 cm.
To save time, take time to check gauge.

Man's Cardigan

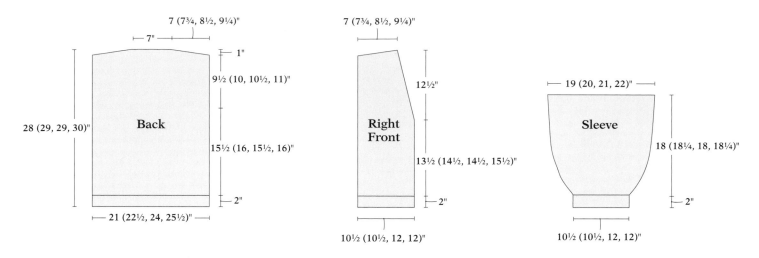

Color Sequence
Same as for Woman's Cardigan.

Bird's-Eye Slip St Patt
Same as for Woman's Cardigan.

Back
With smaller needles and B, CO 84 (90, 96, 102) sts. Change to A, and work K1 P1 rib until piece measures 2"/5 cm from beg. Next Row (WS): Change to larger needles, and purl across. Change to B, and work Bird's-Eye Slip St Patt in Color Sequence until piece measures 27 (28, 28, 29)"/68.5 (71, 71, 73.5) cm from beg.
Shape Shoulders: BO 9 (10, 11, 12) sts at beg of next four rows, then BO 10 (11, 12, 13) sts at beg of next two rows. Slip rem 28 sts onto holder for back of neck.

Pocket Lining (Make Two)
With larger needles and A, CO 22 sts. Work Stockinette St for 5"/12.5 cm, ending after WS row. Slip sts onto holder.

Right Front
With smaller needles and B, CO 42 (42, 48, 48) sts. Change to A, and work K1 P1 rib until piece measures 2"/5 cm from beg. Next Row (WS): Change to larger needles, and purl across. Change to B, and work Bird's-Eye Slip St Patt in Color Sequence until piece measures 7"/18 cm from beg, ending after WS row.
Place Pocket Lining: Next Row (RS): work across first 10 (10, 13, 13) sts, slip next 22 sts onto holder and with RS facing, work patt across 22 sts from one pocket lining, work in Bird's-Eye Slip St Patt to end of row. Cont in patt as established until piece measures 15½ (16½, 16½, 17½)"/39.5 (42, 42, 44.5) cm from beg, ending after WS row.

Shape Neck: Dec 1 st at beg of next row, then every fourth row 5 (0, 5, 0) times, then every sixth row 8 (7, 8, 7) times, then every eighth row 0 (3, 0, 3) times; **and at the same time,** when piece measures same as back to shoulder, **Shape Shoulder** same as for back.

Left Front
Work same as for right front, *except* reverse all shaping and pocket placement.

Sleeves
With smaller needles and B, CO 42 (42, 48, 48) sts. Change to A, and work K1 P1 rib until piece measures 2"/5 cm from beg. Next Row (WS): Change to larger needles, and purl across. Change to B, work Bird's-Eye Slip St

Patt in Color Sequence, and inc 1 st each side every fourth row 3 (9, 6, 12) times, then every sixth row 15 (11, 13, 9) times—78 (82, 86, 90) sts. Cont even until sleeve measures 20 (20¼, 20, 20½)"/51 (51.5, 51, 52) cm from the beg. BO.

Finishing

Pocket Edges: With RS facing, smaller needles, and A, pick up and K22 from pocket holder. Work K1 P1 rib until rib measures ¾"/2 cm. Change to B, work one row rib, then BO in rib.

Sew sides of edges to RS of front. Sew lining to WS of front.
Sew shoulder seams.

Front Bands: With RS facing, circular knitting needle, and A, beg at lower edge of right front, and pick up and K292 (300, 300, 308) along right front edge, around back of neck and down to lower edge of left front. Work K1 P1 rib for ¾"/2 cm. Place markers along left front for six evenly spaced buttonholes, making the first ½"/1.5 cm from bottom and the last ½"/2 cm from beg of neck shaping. Next Row:

BO 3 sts on left front as marked. Next Row: CO 3 sts over the bound-off sts from previous row. Cont in rib until bands measure 1¼"/3 cm, ending after RS row. Next Row: Change to B, and work one row rib as established. BO in rib. With RS facing, crochet hook, and B, work one row of sc along bottom edge of front bands.
Place markers 9½ (10, 10½, 11)"/24 (25.5, 26.5, 28) cm down from shoulders. Set in sleeves between markers. Sew sleeve and side seams. Sew on buttons.

Child's Crew-Neck Pullover

Skill Level
Advanced Beginner

Sizes
Child's size 8 (10, 12, 14). Instructions are for smallest size, with changes for larger sizes noted in parentheses as necessary.

Finished Measurements
Chest: 36 (39, 42, 45)"/91.5 (99, 106.5, 114.5) cm
Length: 18 (19½, 20, 21½)"/45.5 (49.5, 51, 54.5) cm
Sleeve width at upper arm: 15 (16, 17, 18)"/38 (40.5, 43, 45.5) cm

Materials
* JCA/Reynolds's *Lopi* (bulky weight; 100% wool, 3½ oz/100 g; approx 110 yds/100 m), 5 (5, 6, 7) skeins Cherry Red #302 (**A**) and 2 (2, 3, 3) skeins each of Goldenrod #203 (**B**) and Apple Green #212 (**C**)
* Knitting needles, sizes 9 and 10½ (5.5 and 6.5 mm) or size needed to obtain gauge
* 16"/40 cm circular knitting needle, size 9 (5.5 mm)
* Two stitch holders

Gauge
With larger needles in Bird's-Eye Slip St Patt, 16 sts and 24 rows = 4"/10 cm.
To save time, take time to check gauge.

Color Sequence
Same as for Woman's Cardigan.

Bird's-Eye Slip St Patt
Same as for Woman's Cardigan.

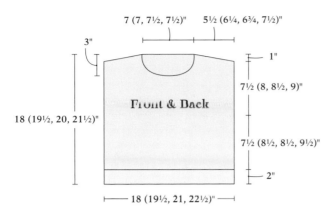

7 (7, 7½, 7½)"   5½ (6¼, 6¾, 7½)"

3"

1"

7½ (8, 8½, 9)"

Front & Back

18 (19½, 20, 21½)"

7½ (8½, 8½, 9½)"

2"

18 (19½, 21, 22½)"

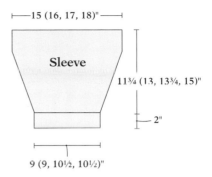

15 (16, 17, 18)"

Sleeve

11¾ (13, 13¾, 15)"

2"

9 (9, 10½, 10½)"

Back

With smaller needles and B, CO 72 (78, 84, 90) sts. Change to A, and work K1 P1 rib until piece measures 2"/5 cm from beg. Next Row (WS): Change to larger needles, and purl across. Change to B and work Bird's-Eye Slip St Patt in Color Sequence until piece measures 17 (18½, 19, 20½)"/43 (47, 48.5, 52) cm from beg.
Shape Shoulders: BO 7 (8, 9, 10) sts at beg of next four rows, then BO 8 (9, 9, 10) sts at beg of next two rows. Slip rem 28 (28, 30, 30) sts onto holder for back of neck.

Front

Work same as back until piece measures 15 (16½, 17, 18½)"/38 (42, 43, 47) cm from beg.
Shape Neck: Work across first 29 (32, 34, 37) sts, slip middle 14 (14, 16, 16) sts onto holder for front of neck, join second skein of yarn and work to end row. Work both sides at once with separate skeins of yarn and BO 3 sts each neck edge once, BO 2 sts each neck edge once, then dec 1 st each neck edge every other row twice; **and at the same time,** when front measures same as back to shoulders, **Shape Shoulders** same as for back.

Sleeves

With smaller needles and A, CO 36 (36, 42, 42) sts. Change to A, and work K1 P1 rib until piece measures 2"/5 cm from beg. Next Row (WS): Change to larger needles, and purl across. Change to B, work Bird's-Eye Slip St Patt in Color Sequence, and inc 1 st each side every fourth row 4 (6, 1, 3) times, then every sixth row 8 (8, 12, 12) times—60 (64, 68, 72) sts. Cont even until sleeve measures 13¾ (15, 15¾, 17)"/35 (38, 40, 43) cm from beg. BO.

Finishing

Sew shoulder seams.
Neckband: With RS facing, circular knitting needle, and A, pick up and K72 (72, 76, 76) around neckline, including sts from neck holders. Work rnds of K1 P1 rib for 1"/2.5 cm. Change to B, work one row in rib, then BO in rib.
Place markers 7½ (8, 8½, 9)"/19 (20.5, 21.5, 23) cm down from shoulders. Set in sleeves between markers. Sew sleeve and side seams.

Harbor View Guernseys

Simple knit and purl stitches, along with an occasional bobble, create wonderful texture in these Guernsey-inspired designs. Don't be intimidated by the woman's bobbled border— it's easy and great fun to knit!

Woman's Rolled-Neck Pullover

Designer Hint

For these projects, select a smooth yarn so that the beautifully textured patterns stand out. Likewise, avoid dark colors, because knit/purl combinations rely on the interplay of light and dark shadows for their effectiveness.

Skill Level
Intermediate

Sizes
Woman's Small (Medium, Large). Instructions are for smallest size, with changes for other sizes noted in parentheses as necessary.

Finished Measurements
Bust: 40 (44, 48)"/101.5 (112, 122) cm
Length: 20½ (21, 22)"/52 (53.5, 56) cm
Sleeve width at upper arm: 17 (18, 19)"/43 (45.5, 48.5) cm

Materials
- Spinrite/Bernat's *Berella 4* (worsted weight; 100% acrylic with Bounce-Back® fibers; 3½ oz/100 g; approx 240 yds/219 m), 6 (7, 8) skeins Medium Teal #8844
- Knitting needles, sizes 5, 6, and 7 (3.75, 4, and 4.5 mm) or size needed to obtain gauge
- Two stitch holders

Gauge
With largest needles in Woman's Guernsey Patt, 20 sts and 30 rows = 4"/10 cm. **To save time, take time to check gauge.**

Back
With size 6 needles, CO 101 (111, 121) sts. Work Woman's Guernsey Border Patt Rows 1 to 10. Change to largest needles, beg and end where indicated, and work Woman's Guernsey Patt until piece measures 19½ (20, 21)"/49.5 (51, 53.5) cm from beg.
Shape Shoulders: BO 8 (9, 10) sts at beg of next six rows, then BO 8 (10, 12) sts at beg of next two rows. Slip rem 37 sts onto holder for back of neck.

Front
Work same as back until piece measures 18 (18½, 19½)"/45.5 (47, 49.5) cm from beg.
Shape Neck: Work across first 43 (48, 53) sts, slip middle 15 sts onto holder for front of neck; join second skein of yarn and work to end row. Work both sides at once with separate skeins of yarn, and BO 3 sts each neck edge twice, BO 2 sts each neck edge once, then dec 1 st each neck edge every other row three times; **and at the same time,** when front measures same as back to shoulders, **Shape Shoulders** same as for back.

Sleeves
With size 6 needles, CO 51 sts. Work Woman's Guernsey Border Patt Rows 1 to 10. Change to largest needles, beg and end where indicated, work Woman's Guernsey Patt, and inc 1 st each side every fourth row 0 (2, 8) times, then every sixth row 8 (18, 14)

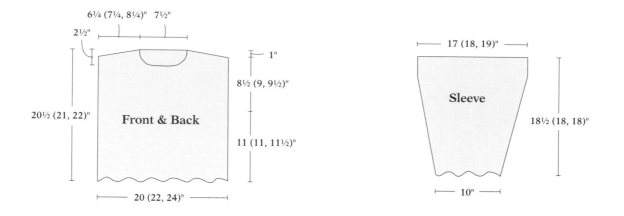

6¼ (7¼, 8¼)" 7½"

2½"

1"

8½ (9, 9½)"

20½ (21, 22)"

Front & Back

11 (11, 11½)"

20 (22, 24)"

17 (18, 19)"

Sleeve

18½ (18, 18)"

10"

times, then every eighth row 9 (0, 0) times—85 (91, 95) sts. Cont even until sleeve measures 18½ (18, 18)"/47 (45.5, 45.5) cm from beg. BO.

Finishing

Sew left shoulder seam.

Neckband: With RS facing and size 6 needles, pick up and K84 along neckline, including sts from neck holders. Work Rows 1 to 3 of Woman's Guernsey Patt. Change to smallest needles and work Stockinette St for 1"/2.5 cm, ending after WS row. BO knitwise, allowing band to roll to RS. Sew right shoulder seam, including side of neckband. Place markers 8½ (9, 9½)"/21.5 (23, 24) cm down from shoulders. Set in sleeves between markers. Sew sleeve and side seams.

Woman's Guernsey Patt

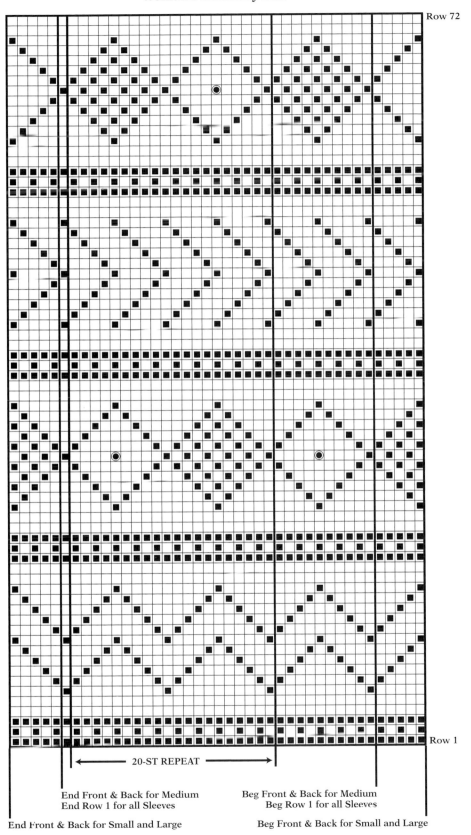

Row 72

Row 1

← 20-ST REPEAT →

End Front & Back for Medium
End Row 1 for all Sleeves

Beg Front & Back for Medium
Beg Row 1 for all Sleeves

End Front & Back for Small and Large

Beg Front & Back for Small and Large

Woman's Guernsey Border Patt

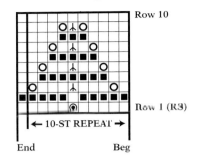

Row 10

Row 1 (RS)

← 10-ST REPEAT →

End   Beg

Key

☐ = Knit on RS; purl on WS

■ = Purl on RS; knit on WS

◉ = Bobble. (K1, yarn over) four times into
next st, K1 again into same st; P5, turn;
K5, turn; p2tog, P1, p2tog, turn; slip 1 st
knitwise, k2tog, psso

Ⓞ = Yarn over

⼈ = Slip 1 st; k2tog; psso

Man's Cardigan Vest

Skill Level
Intermediate

Sizes
Man's Small (Medium, Large, Extra-Large). Instructions are for smallest size, with changes for other sizes noted in parentheses as necessary.

Finished Measurements
Chest (Buttoned): 40 (44, 48, 52)"/101.5 (112, 122, 132) cm
Length: 25 (26, 26, 27)"/63.5 (66, 66, 68.5) cm

Materials
* Spinrite/Bernat's *Berella 4* (worsted weight; 100% acrylic with Bounce-Back® fibers; 3½ oz/100 g; approx 240 yds/219 m), 5 (5, 6, 7) skeins Medium Olive #8882
* Knitting needles, sizes 6 and 7 (4 and 4.5 mm) or size needed to obtain gauge
* 16"/40 cm circular knitting needle, size 6 (4 mm)
* Three stitch holders
* Five 1"/25 mm buttons (JHB International's *Leather-All* style #60335 in Brown was used in sample garment)

Gauge
With larger needles in Man's Guernsey Patt, 20 sts and 30 rows = 4"/10 cm. **To save time, take time to check gauge.**

Back
With larger needles, CO 101 (111, 121, 131) sts. Work K1 P1 rib for 1½"/4 cm. Beg and end where indicated, work Man's Guernsey Patt until piece measures 13½ (14½, 14, 15)"/34.5 (37, 35.5, 38) cm from beg.

Shape Armholes: BO 3 (4, 5, 6) sts at beg of next two rows, then BO 2 (2, 3, 3) sts at beg of next four rows. Dec 1 st each side every other row 3 (6, 5, 6) times—81 (83, 89, 95) sts rem. Cont even until armholes measure 10½ (10½, 11, 11)"/26.5 (26.5, 28, 28) cm.

Shape Shoulders: BO 6 (6, 7, 7) sts at beg of next six rows, then BO 5 (5, 5, 6) sts at beg of next two rows. BO rem 35 (37, 37, 41) sts.

Pocket Lining (Make Two)

With larger needles, CO 26 (27, 26, 27) sts. Work Stockinette St for 5"/13 cm, ending after WS row. Slip sts onto holder.

Right Front

With larger needles, CO 46 (51, 56, 61) sts. Work K1 P1 rib for 1½"/4 cm. Beg and end where indicated, work Man's Guernsey Patt until piece measures 6½"/16.5 cm from beg, ending after WS row.

Place Pocket Linings: Work across first 10 (12, 15, 17) sts, slip next 26 (27, 26, 27) sts onto holder, cont in patt across 26 (27, 26, 27) sts from one pocket lining holder, work to end of row. Cont even until piece measures 13½ (14½, 14, 15)"/34.5 (37, 35.5, 38) cm from beg, ending after RS row.

Shape Armhole (WS): BO 3 (4, 5, 6) sts at beg of next row.

Shape Neck (RS): Dec 1 st at beg of next row and then again every fourth row 0 (2, 0, 6) more times, then every sixth row 12 (11, 13, 9) times; **and at the same time,** cont to shape armhole at side edge same as for back, and when piece measures same as back to shoulders, **Shape Shoulder** same as for back.

Man's Guernsey Patt

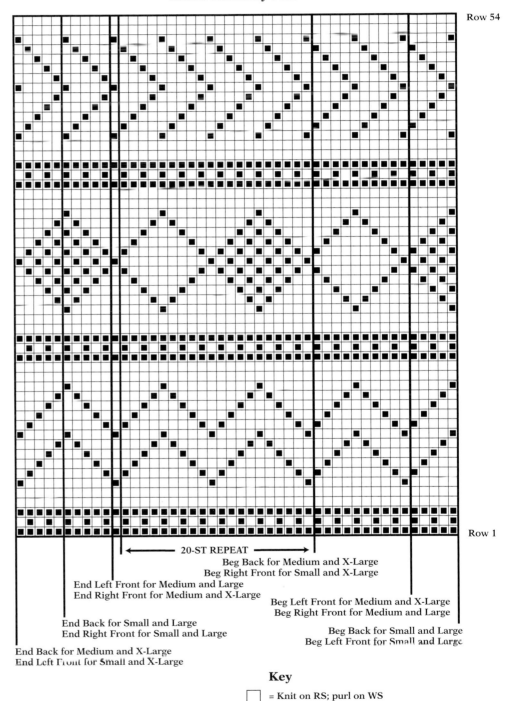

Row 54

Row 1

←——— 20-ST REPEAT ———→

Beg Back for Medium and X-Large
Beg Right Front for Small and X-Large

End Left Front for Medium and Large
End Right Front for Medium and X-Large

Beg Left Front for Medium and X-Large
Beg Right Front for Medium and Large

End Back for Small and Large
End Right Front for Small and Large

Beg Back for Small and Large
Beg Left Front for Small and Large

End Back for Medium and X-Large
End Left Front for Small and X-Large

Key

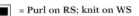

☐ = Knit on RS; purl on WS

■ = Purl on RS; knit on WS

Left Front

Work same as for right front, *except* reverse all shaping and pocket placement.

Finishing

Sew shoulder and side seams.

Front Bands: With RS facing and circular knitting needle, pick up and K148 (152, 152, 156) along right front edge to right shoulder seam, 36 (38, 38, 42) sts along back of neck, and 148 (152, 152, 156) sts along left front edge—332 (342, 342, 354) sts total. Work K1 P1 rib for ¾"/2 cm. Place markers along left front edge for five evenly spaced buttonholes, making the first ½"/1.5 cm from bottom and the last ½"/1.5 cm from beg of neck shaping. Next Row: Cont in rib as established, BO 5 sts for buttonholes where marked. Next Row: CO 5 sts over the bound-off sts from previous row. Cont in rib until band measures 1½"/4 cm from beg, ending after WS row. Next three rows: Work Rows 1 to 3 of Man's Guernsey Patt. BO.

Armhole Bands: With RS facing and circular knitting needle, pick up and K124 (124, 134, 134) around armhole. Join and work K1 P1 rib for 1"/2.5 cm, working a double decrease at side seam every rnd. BO in rib.

Pocket Edges: With RS facing and smaller needles, pick up and knit sts from pocket holder. Work K1 P1 rib for 1"/2.5 cm. BO in rib. Sew pocket linings to WS of fronts. Sew pocket edges to RS of fronts.
Sew on buttons.

Man's Cardigan Vest

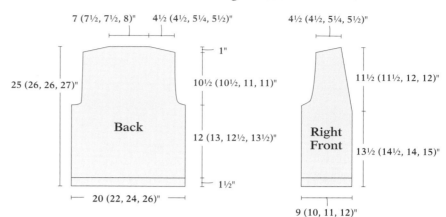

Child's Rolled-Neck Pullover

Skill Level
Advanced Beginner

Sizes
Child's size 2 (4, 6, 8). Instructions are for smallest size, with changes for other sizes noted in parentheses as necessary.

Finished Measurements
Chest: 28 (30, 32, 34)"/71 (76, 81.5, 86.5) cm
Length: 16 (18, 20, 21)"/40.5 (45.5, 51, 53.5) cm
Sleeve width at upper arm: 13 (14, 15, 16)"/33 (35.5, 38, 40.5) cm

Materials
* Spinrite/Bernat's *Berella 4* (worsted weight; 100% acrylic with Bounce-Back® fibers; 3½ oz/100 g; approx 240 yds/219 m), 4 (4, 4, 5) skeins Light Periwinkle #8803
* Knitting needles, sizes 5, 6, and 7 (3.75, 4, and 4.5 mm) or size needed to obtain gauge
* Two stitch holders

Gauge
With largest needles in Stockinette St, 20 sts and 28 rows = 4"/10 cm. **To save time, take time to check gauge.**

Child's Rolled-Neck Pullover

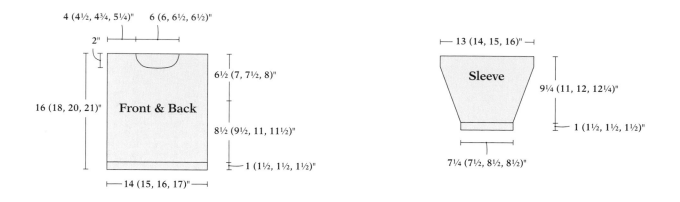

Back

With size 6 needles, CO 71 (77, 81, 87) sts. Work K1 P1 rib for 1 (1½, 1½, 1½)"/2.5 (4 , 4, 4) cm. Change to largest needles and work Stockinette St until piece measures 6¾ (8¼, 9¾, 10¼)"/17 (21, 25, 26) cm from beg, ending after WS row. Beg and end Guernsey Yoke Patt where indicated, and work Rows 1 to 43 once, then repeat Rows 24 to 43 until piece measures 16 (18, 20, 21)"/40.5 (45.5, 51, 53.5) cm from beg. BO 20 (23, 24, 27) sts at beg of next two rows. Slip rem 31 (31, 33, 33) sts onto holder for back of neck.

Front

Work same as for back until piece measures 14 (16, 18, 19)"/35.5 (40.5, 46, 48.5) cm from beg.

Shape Neck: Work across first 29 (32, 33, 36) sts, slip middle 13 (13, 15, 15) sts onto holder for front of neck; join second skein of yarn and work to end row. Work both sides at once with separate skeins, and BO 3 sts each neck edge once, BO 2 sts each neck edge twice, then dec 1 st each neck edge every other row twice. Work even until piece measures same as back to shoulder. BO rem 20 (23, 24, 27) sts.

Sleeves

With size 6 needles, CO 37 (39, 43, 43) sts. Work K1 P1 rib for 1 (1½, 1½, 1½)"/2.5 (4 , 4, 4) cm. Change to largest needles, beg Stockinette St, and inc 1 st each side every other row 7 (5, 3, 7) times, then every fourth row 7 (11, 14, 12) times—65 (71, 77, 81) sts. Cont even until sleeve measures 7¼ (9½, 10½, 10¾)"/18.5 (24, 26.5, 27.5) cm from beg, ending after WS row. Work Rows 1 to 21 of Guernsey Yoke Patt. BO.

Finishing

Sew left shoulder seam.
Neckband: With RS facing and size 6 needles, pick up and K78 (78, 82, 82) around neckline, including sts from front and back neck holders. Work Rows 1 to 3 of Guernsey Yoke Patt. Change to smallest needles and work Stockinette St for 1½"/4 cm ending after WS row. BO knitwise **loosely,** allowing band to roll to RS.
Sew right shoulder seam, including side of neckband. Place markers 6½ (7, 7½, 8)"/16.5 (18, 19, 20.5) cm down from shoulders. Set in sleeves between markers. Sew sleeve and side seams.

Guernsey Yoke Patt

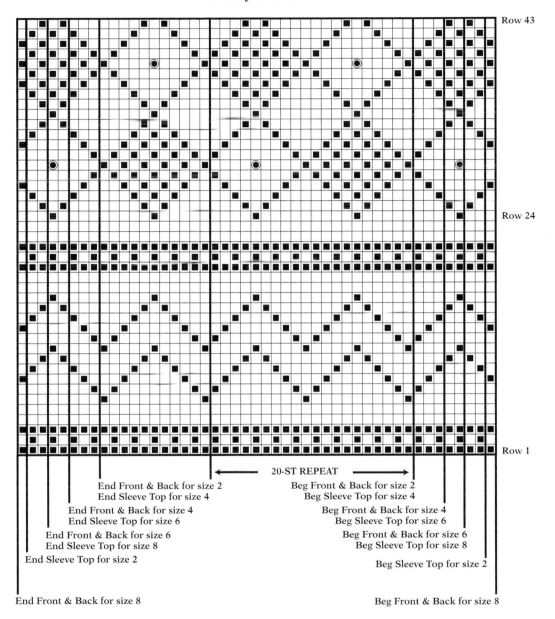

Row 43

Row 24

Row 1

← 20-ST REPEAT →

End Front & Back for size 2
End Sleeve Top for size 4

Beg Front & Back for size 2
Beg Sleeve Top for size 4

End Front & Back for size 4
End Sleeve Top for size 6

Beg Front & Back for size 4
Beg Sleeve Top for size 6

End Front & Back for size 6
End Sleeve Top for size 8

Beg Front & Back for size 6
Beg Sleeve Top for size 8

End Sleeve Top for size 2

Beg Sleeve Top for size 2

End Front & Back for size 8

Beg Front & Back for size 8

Key

☐ = Knit on RS; purl on WS

■ = Purl on RS; knit on WS

◉ = Bobble: (K1, yarn over) four times into next st, K1 again into same st; P5, turn; K5, turn; p2tog, P1, p2tog, turn; slip 1 st knitwise, k2tog, psso

Argyle
Antics

Vibrant colors and interesting pattern placement

lend whimsical twists to the traditional argyle.

For even more fun, the woman's and child's versions

feature color blocking.

Woman's Crew-Neck Pullover

Designer Hint

When working the hollow diamonds of argyle charts, such as the gold stitches in the Man's V-Neck Vest, work the first stitch from the middle of a long length of yarn, leaving two tails. This way, you will have two available strands of yarn to knit with on subsequent rows, one for each side of the diamond.

Skill Level

Intermediate

Sizes

Woman's Small (Medium, Large, Extra-Large). Instructions are for smallest size, with changes for other sizes noted in parentheses as necessary.

Finished Measurements

Bust: 36 (38, 40, 42)"/91.5 (96.5, 101.5, 106.5) cm

Hip: 32 (34, 36, 38)"/81.5 (86.5, 91.5, 96.5) cm

Length: 18 (19, 20, 20)"/45.5 (48.5, 51, 51) cm

Sleeve width at upper arm: 14 (14¾, 15½, 15½)"/35.5 (37.5, 39.5, 39.5) cm

Materials

- Westminster Fibers/Rowan's *Handknit DK Cotton* (light worsted weight; 100% cotton, 1¾ oz/50 g; approx 90 yds/85 m), 4 (5, 5, 6) balls Basil #221 (**A**); 4 (4, 5, 6) balls Scarlet #255 (**B**); and 1 ball each of Gooseberry #219 (**C**), Sunkissed #231 (**D**), and Grape #211 (**E**)
- Knitting needles, sizes 5 and 6 (3.75 and 4 mm) or size needed to obtain gauge
- 16"/40 cm circular knitting needle, size 5 (3.75 mm)
- Two stitch holders
- Bobbins

Gauge

With larger needles in Stockinette St, 21 sts and 28 rows = 4"/10 cm. **To save time, take time to check gauge.**

Back

With smaller needles and A, CO 85 (89, 95, 99) sts. Work K1 P1 rib for 1"/2.5 cm. Change to larger needles, beg Stockinette St, and inc 1 st each side every eighth row 5 (5, 5, 6) times—95 (99, 105, 111) sts. Cont even until piece measures 9½ (10, 10½, 10½)"/24 (25.5, 26.5, 26.5) cm from beg, ending after WS row.

Shape Armholes: BO 4 (5, 5, 6) sts at beg of next two rows. Next Row (RS): ssk, K6 (7, 10, 12), work Row 1 of Horizontal Argyle Patt over middle 71 sts, K6 (7, 10, 12), k2tog. Cont this way, and dec 1 st each side every other row 4 (4, 4, 5) more times, working B

on sts either side of chart after Row 15 is completed, and on all sts after Row 30 of chart is completed—77 (79, 85, 87) sts rem. Cont even until armholes measure 7½ (8, 8½, 8½)"/19 (20.5, 21.5, 21.5) cm.

Shape Shoulders: BO 5 sts at beg of next six rows, then BO 4 (5, 6, 7) sts at beg of next two rows. Slip rem 39 (39, 43, 43) sts onto holder for back of neck.

Front

Work same as back until armholes measure 5½ (6, 6½, 6½)"/14 (15, 16.5, 16.5) cm.

Shape Neck: Work across first 30 (31, 32, 33) sts, slip middle 17 (17, 21, 21) sts onto holder for front of neck; join second ball of yarn and work to end of row. Work both sides at once with separate balls of yarn, and BO 3 sts each neck edge twice, BO 2 sts each neck edge once, then dec 1 st each neck edge every other row three times; **and at the same time,** when front measures same as back to shoulders, **Shape Shoulders** same as for back.

Sleeves

With smaller needles and B, CO 63 (63, 65, 65) sts. Work K1 P1 rib for 1"/2.5 cm. Change to larger needles, beg Stockinette St, and inc 1 st each side every row 0 (2, 4, 4) times, then every other row 5 (5, 4, 4) times—73 (77, 81, 81) sts. Cont even until sleeve measures 3½"/9 cm from beg.

Shape Cap: BO 4 (5, 5, 6) sts at beg of next two rows, then dec 1 st each side every fourth row 0 (0, 0, 1) times, then every other row 11 (14, 16, 14) times, then every row 2 (0, 0, 0) times. BO 4 sts at beg of next four rows. BO the rem 23 sts.

Finishing

Sew shoulder seams.

Neckband: With RS facing, circular knitting needle, and B, pick up and K90 (90, 98, 98) around neckline, including sts from neck holders. Work rnds of K1 P1 rib for 1"/2.5 cm. BO in rib.

Set in sleeves. Sew sleeve and side seams.

Woman's Crew-Neck Pullover

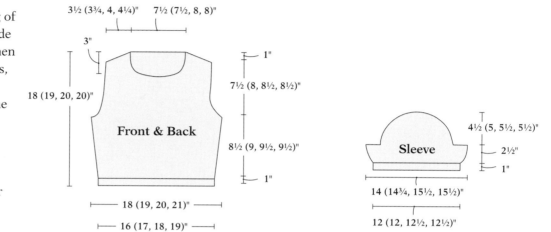

Horizontal Argyle Patt

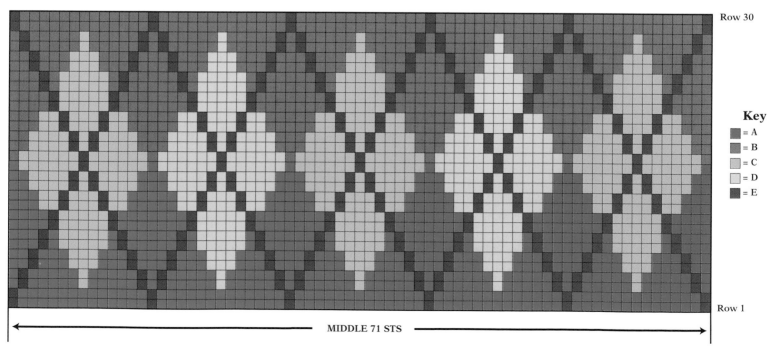

Key
- = A
- = B
- = C
- = D
- = E

Man's V-Neck Vest

Skill Level
Intermediate

Sizes
Man's Small (Medium, Large, Extra-Large). Instructions are for smallest size, with changes for other sizes noted in parentheses as necessary.

Finished Measurements
Chest: 41 (44, 47, 50)"/104 (112, 119.5, 127) cm

Length: 25¾ (25¾, 27, 27)"/65.5 (65.5, 68.5, 68.5) cm

Materials
- Westminster Fibers/Rowan's *Handknit DK Cotton* (light worsted weight; 100% cotton, 1¾ oz/50 g; approx 90 yds/85 m), 9 (10, 11, 12) balls Grape #211 (**A**) and 1 ball each of Scarlet #255 (**B**), Gooseberry #219 (**C**), and Sunkissed #231 (**D**)
- Knitting needles, size 6 (4 mm) or size needed to obtain gauge
- 16"/40 cm circular knitting needle, size 5 (3.75 mm)
- Two stitch holders
- Bobbins

Gauge
In Stockinette St, 21 sts and 28 rows = 4"/10 cm. **To save time, take time to check gauge.**

Back
With A, CO 109 (117, 125, 133) sts. Work K1 P1 rib for 2"/5 cm. Work Stockinette St until piece measures 14¼ (14¼, 15, 15)"/36 (36, 38, 38) cm from beg.

Shape Armholes: BO 3 (4, 4, 4) sts at beg of next four rows, then BO 2 (2, 2, 3) sts at beg of next four rows, then dec

1 st each side every other row three times—83 (87, 95, 99) sts rem. Cont even until armholes measure 10½ (10½, 11, 11)"/26.5 (26.5, 28, 28) cm.

Shape Shoulders: BO 6 (6, 7, 7) sts at

beg of next four rows, then BO 5 (6, 6, 7) sts at beg of next four rows. Slip rem 39 (39, 43, 43) sts onto holder for back of neck.

Front

Work same as back until piece measures 2"/5 cm from beg. Next Row (RS) K33 (37, 41, 45), work Row 1 of Vertical Argyle Patt over middle 43 sts, work to end row. Cont even in patt as established until piece measures same as back to underarm. **Shape Armholes:** Same as for back. Cont even until armholes measure 3½ (3½, 3, 3)"/9 (9, 7.5, 7.5) cm. **Shape Neck:** Work across first 39 (41, 45, 47) sts, k2tog, slip next st onto holder or safety pin for front of neck; join second ball of yarn and ssk, work to end of row. Work both sides at once with separate balls of yarn, and dec 1 st each neck edge every other row 10 (10, 11, 11) times, then every fourth row 8 (8, 9, 9) times, working all sts in A after Row 44 of Vertical Argyle Patt is completed for the second time; **and at the same time,** when front measures same as back to shoulders, **Shape Shoulders** same as for back.

Finishing

Sew shoulder seams.

Neckband: With RS facing, circular knitting needle, and A, beg at right shoulder and pick up and K39 (39, 43, 43) from back neck holder, 45 (45, 47, 47) sts along left front neck, K1 from front neck holder and mark it, pick up and K45 (45, 47, 47) along right neck edge—130 (130, 138, 138) sts total. Place marker, join, and work rnds of K1 P1 rib with mitered decrease at center of front as follows: Work to 2 sts before marked st at center front, ssk, knit center st, k2tog, work to end of rnd. When band measures 1"/2.5 cm from beg, BO in rib.

Armbands: With RS facing, circular knitting needle, and A, pick up and K118 (118, 122, 122) around armhole. Work K1 P1 rib for 1"/2.5 cm. BO in rib. Sew side seams.

Man's V-Neck Vest

7½ (7½, 8, 8)"   4 (4½, 5, 5½)"

8 (8, 9, 9)"

1"

10½ (10½, 11, 11)"

25¾ (25¾, 27, 27)"

Front & Back

12¼ (12¼, 13, 13)"

2"

20½ (22, 23½, 25)"

Vertical Argyle Patt

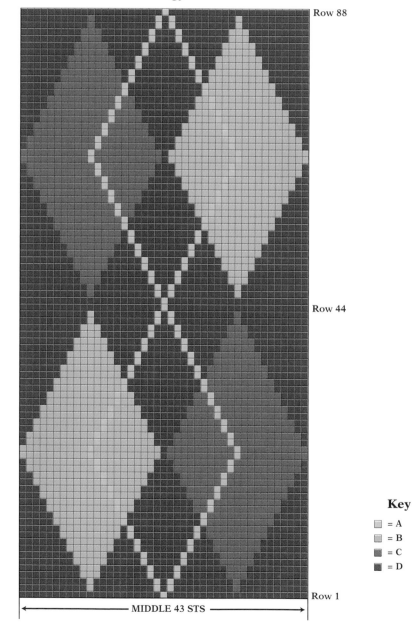

Row 88

Row 44

Row 1

MIDDLE 43 STS

Key

■ = A
■ = B
■ = C
■ = D

Child's Color-Block Pullover

Skill Level
Intermediate

Sizes
Child's 8 (10, 12, 14). Instructions are for smallest size, with changes for other sizes noted in parentheses as necessary.

Finished Measurements
Chest: 35 (36½, 38½, 40)"/89 (92.5, 98, 101.5) cm

Length: 17½ (18, 19, 20)"/44.5 (45.5, 48.5, 51) cm

Sleeve width at upper arm: 14 (15, 16, 17)"/35.5 (38, 40.5, 43) cm

Materials
• Westminster Fibers/Rowan's *Handknit DK Cotton* (light worsted weight; 100% cotton, 1¾ oz/50 g; approx 90 yds/85 m), 2 (3, 4, 4) balls Sunkissed #231 (**A**); 4 (5, 6, 7) balls each of Grape #211 (**B**) and Scarlet #255 (**C**); and 1 (1, 2, 2) ball each of Gooseberry #219 (**D**) and Basil #221 (**E**)
• Knitting needles, sizes 5 and 6 (3.75 and 4 mm) or size needed to obtain gauge
• 16"/40 cm circular knitting needle, size 5 (3.75 mm)
• Two stitch holders
• Bobbins

Gauge
With larger needles in Stockinette St, 21 sts and 28 rows = 4"/10 cm. **To save time, take time to check gauge.**

Child's Color-Block Pullover

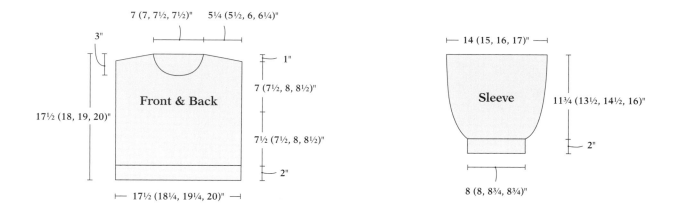

Back

With smaller needles and A, CO 92 (96, 102, 106) sts. Establish rib as follows: *For size 8 only:* P1, *K2, P2. Repeat from * across, ending row with K2, P1. *For size 10 only:* K1, *P2, K2. Repeat from * across, ending row with P2, K1. *For size 12 only:* *P2, K2. Repeat from * across, ending row with P2. *For size 14 only:* *K2, P2. Repeat from * across, ending row with K2. *For all sizes:* Work rib as established until piece measures 2"/5 cm from beg. Next Row (WS): Change to larger needles and B, and purl across first 45 (47, 50, 52) sts; join A and P2; join C and purl to end row. Next Row (RS): K26 (28, 31, 33) with C, work Row 1 of Color-Block Argyle Patt across middle 40 sts, knit with B to end row. Cont working patt as established until piece measures 16½ (17, 18, 19)"/42 (43, 45.5, 48.5) cm from beg.

Shape Shoulders: BO 7 (7, 8, 8) sts at beg of next four rows, then BO 7 (8, 8, 9) sts at beg of next four rows. Slip rem 36 (36, 38, 38) sts onto holder for back of neck.

Front

Work same as back until piece measures 14½ (15, 16, 17)"/37 (38, 40.5, 43) cm from beg.

Shape Neck: Work across first 39 (41, 44, 46) sts, slip middle 14 sts onto holder for front of neck; join second ball of yarn and work to end of row. Work both sides at once with separate balls of yarn, and BO 3 (3, 4, 4) sts each neck edge once, BO 2 sts each neck edge twice, then dec 1 st each neck edge every other row four times; **and at the same time,** when front measures same as back to shoulders, **Shape Shoulders** same as for back.

Left Sleeve

With smaller needles and A, CO 42 (42, 46, 46) sts. Work K2 P2 rib for 2"/5 cm. Next Row (WS): Change to larger needles and B, and purl across first 21 (21, 23, 23) sts; join C and purl to end row. Cont in colors as established, and inc 1 st each side every fourth row 11 (11, 10, 14) times, then every sixth row 5 (7, 9, 8) times—74 (78, 84, 90) sts. Cont even until sleeve measures 13¾ (15½, 16½, 18)"/35 (39.5, 42, 45.5) cm from beg. BO.

Right Sleeve

With smaller needles and A, CO 42 (42, 46, 46) sts. Work same as for left sleeve, *except* reverse colors B and C.

Finishing

Sew shoulder seams.

Neckband: With RS facing, circular knitting needle, and A, pick up and K80 (80, 84, 84) around neckline, including sts from neck holders. Work rnds of K2 P2 rib for 1"/2.5 cm. BO loosely in rib.

Place markers 7 (7½, 8, 8½)"/18 (19, 20.5, 21.5) cm down from shoulders. Set in sleeves between markers. Sew sleeve and side seams.

Color-Block Argyle Patt

Row 80

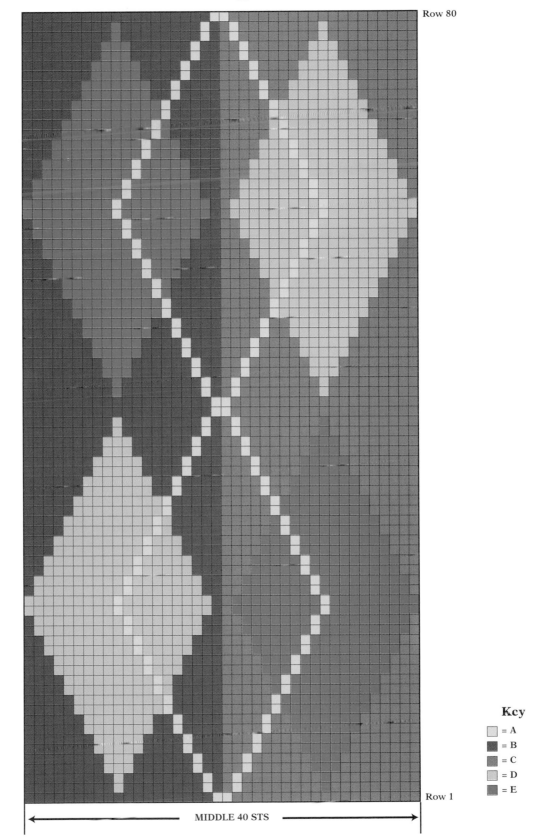

Row 1

MIDDLE 40 STS

Kcy

☐ = A
■ = B
■ = C
☐ = D
■ = E

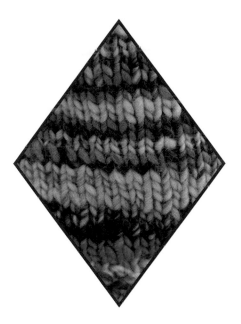

Quick
and Cozy

Let the yarn do all the hard work! Multicolored
yarn in simple Stockinette Stitch yields fantastic
results. The shapes—an oversized casual
cardigan, a basic pullover, and a fun swing coat—
are wonderfully wearable.

Woman's Shawl-Collar Cardigan

Skill Level
Advanced Beginner

Sizes
Woman's Small (Medium, Large, Extra-Large). Instructions are for smallest size, with changes for other sizes noted in parentheses as necessary.

Finished Measurements
Bust (Buttoned): 40 (43¼, 47, 50)"/101.5 (109, 119.5, 127) cm
Length: 29 (30, 30, 31)"/73.5 (76, 76, 78.5) cm
Sleeve width at upper arm: 18 (19, 19, 20)"/45.5 (48.5, 48.5, 51) cm

Materials
* Muench's *Naturwolle* (bulky weight; 100% wool; 3½ oz/100 g; approx 110 yds/100 m), 12 (13, 13, 14) hanks Karibik #23
* Knitting needles, size 10½ (6.5 mm) or size needed to obtain gauge
* Two stitch holders
* Seven 1⅛"/28 mm buttons (JHB International's *Rushmore* style #86831 in Marbled Beige was used on sample garment)

Gauge
In Stockinette St, 13 sts and 18 rows = 4"/10 cm. **To save time, take time to check gauge.**

Note
Instructions include one selvage st each side; these sts are not reflected in finished measurements.

Designer Hint

When knitting with novelty yarn, use a smooth yarn in a complementary color for seaming up the garment. Make sure both yarns have the same laundering instructions.

Seed St (multiple of 2 sts plus 1 st)

Row 1 (RS): *K1, P1. Repeat from * across, ending row with K1.
Row 2: Work same as Row 1.
Repeat Rows 1 and 2 for patt.

Back

CO 67 (73, 77, 83) sts. Work Seed St for 2"/5 cm. Beg Stockinette St, and work even until piece measures 18¾ (19¼, 19¼, 19¾)"/47.5 (49, 49, 50) cm from beg.

Shape Armholes: Dec 1 st each side every row three times, then every other row twice—57 (63, 67, 73) sts rem. Cont even until armholes measure 9 (9½, 9½, 10)"/23 (24, 24, 25.5) cm.

Shape Shoulders: BO 6 (7, 7, 8) sts at beg of next four rows, then BO 5 (6, 8, 9) sts at beg of next two rows. BO rem 23 sts.

Pocket Lining (Make Two)

CO 19 sts. Work Stockinette St for 6"/15 cm, ending after WS row. Slip sts onto holder.

Left Front

CO 37 (39, 43, 45) sts. Work Seed St for 2"/5 cm. Next Row (RS): K30 (32, 36, 38), place marker, work Seed St to end row. Cont in Stockinette St with Seed St over 7 front band sts as established until piece measures 8"/20.5 cm from beg, ending after a WS row.

Place Pocket Linings: Work across first 5 (6, 8, 9) sts, slip next 19 sts onto holder, work across 19 sts from one pocket lining holder, work to end row. Work even until piece measures 18¾ (19¼, 19¼, 19¾)"/47.5 (49, 49, 50) cm from beg, ending after WS row.

Shape Armhole: Dec 1 st at armhole edge every row three times, then every other row twice. Cont even until piece measures 22 (23, 23, 24)"/56 (58.5, 58.5, 61) cm from beg, ending after a RS row.

Shape Neck: Work across first 7 sts and slip them onto holder, k2tog, work to end row. Dec 1 st at neck edge every

other row 1 (0, 3, 1) more times, then every fourth row 6 (6, 5, 6) times; **and at the same time,** when piece measures same as back to shoulders, **Shape Shoulders** same as for back. Place markers along front band for seven evenly spaced buttons, making the first ½"/1.5 cm from bottom and the last ½"/1.5 cm from beg of neck shaping.

Right Front

Work same as for left front, *except* reverse all shaping and pocket placement, and make seven 3-st buttonholes by working (K1, P1, BO 3 sts) at beg of RS rows opposite markers. On next row, CO 3 sts over the bound-off sts from previous row.

Sleeves

CO 35 (35, 39, 39) sts. Work Seed St for 2"/5 cm. Beg Stockinette St, and inc 1 st each side every fourth row 5 (8, 2, 8) times, then every sixth row 8 (6, 10, 6) times—61 (63, 63, 67) sts. Cont even until sleeve measures 18"/45.5 cm from the beg.

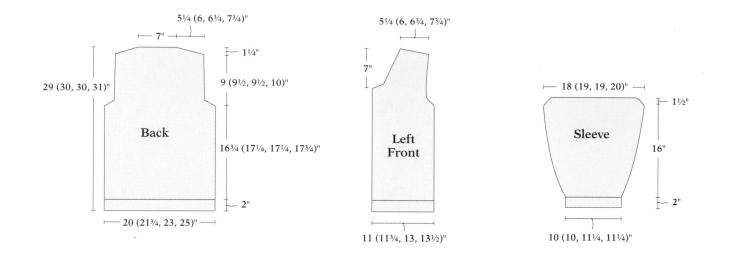

Back
5¼ (6, 6¾, 7¾)"
7"
1¼"
9 (9½, 9½, 10)"
29 (30, 30, 31)"
16¾ (17¼, 17¼, 17¾)"
2"
20 (21¾, 23, 25)"

Left Front
5¼ (6, 6¾, 7¾)"
7"
11 (11¾, 13, 13½)"

Sleeve
18 (19, 19, 20)"
1½"
16"
2"
10 (10, 11¼, 11¼)"

Shape Cap: Work same as back armhole shaping. BO rem 51 (53, 53, 57) sts.

Finishing

Sew shoulder seams.

Pocket Edgings: With RS facing and smaller needles, pick up and knit sts from lining holders. Work Seed St for 1"/2.5 cm. BO. Sew sides of pocket edge to front. Sew pocket linings to WS of front.

Collar: Continuing on sts from one front band holder, work Seed St and inc 1 st each side every row four times, then every other row three times. Inc 1 st each side every fourth row once, then every sixth row twice—27 sts. Cont even for 5"/12.5 cm more. Slip sts onto holder. Repeat for other band. Weave sts tog at back of neck. Sew collar into place along front neck shaping and back of neck.

Set in sleeves. Sew sleeve and side seams. Sew on buttons.

Man's Crew-Neck Pullover

Skill Level
Beginner

Sizes
Man's Small (Medium, Large, Extra-Large). Instructions are for smallest size, with changes for other sizes noted in parentheses as necessary.

Finished Measurements
Chest: 44 (48½, 52, 56)"/112 (123, 132, 142) cm

Length: 26 (27, 27½, 28)"/66 (68.5, 70, 71) cm

Sleeve width at upper arm: 19 (20, 21, 22)"/48.5 (51, 53.5, 56) cm

Materials
* Muench's *Naturwolle* (bulky weight; 100% wool; 3½ oz/100 g; approx 110 yds/100 m), 1 (1, 1, 2) hank Black Forest Brown #U42 (**A**) and 10 (10, 11, 12) hanks Rust #304 (**B**)
* Knitting needles, size 10½ (6.5 mm) or size needed to obtain gauge
* 16"/40 cm circular knitting needle, size 10 (6 mm)
* Two stitch holders

Gauge
In Stockinette St, 13 sts and 18 rows = 4"/10 cm. **To save time, take time to check gauge.**

Man's Crew-Neck Pullover

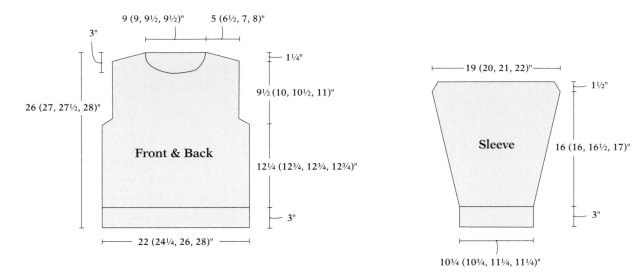

Note

Instructions include 1 selvage st each side; these sts are not reflected in finished measurements.

Back

With A, CO 73 (81, 87, 93) sts. Work one row K1 P1 rib. *Next Row (WS): Change to B, and purl across. Work K1 P1 rib for three rows. Next Row (WS): Change to A, and purl across. Next Row: Work rib as established. Repeat from * once more. Next Row: Change to B, and purl across. Cont in rib until piece measures 3"/7.5 cm from beg. Work even in Stockinette St with B until piece measures 15¼ (15¾, 15¾, 15¾)"/38.5 (40, 40, 40) cm from beg.

Shape Armholes: Dec 1 st each side every row three times, then dec 1 st each side every other row twice—63 (71, 77, 83) sts rem. Cont even until armholes measure 9½ (10, 10½, 11)"/24 (25.5, 26.5, 28) cm.

Shape Shoulders: BO 6 (7, 8, 9) sts at beg of next four rows, then BO 5 (7, 7, 8) sts at beg of next two rows. Slip rem 29 (29, 31, 31) sts onto holder for back of neck.

Front

Work same as back until armholes measure 7¾ (8¼, 8¾, 9¼)"/19.5 (21, 22, 23.5) cm.

Shape Neck: Work across first 26 (30, 32, 35) sts, slip middle 11 (11, 13, 13) sts onto holder for front of neck; join second ball of yarn and work to end of row. Work both sides at once with separate balls of yarn, and BO 3 sts each neck edge once, BO 2 sts each neck edge twice, then dec 1 st each neck edge every other row twice; **and at the same time,** when front measures same as back to shoulders, **Shape Shoulders** same as for back.

Sleeves

With A, CO 37 (37, 39, 39) sts. Work same as back until piece measures 3"/7.5 cm from beg. Beg Stockinette St, and inc 1 st each side every fourth row 5 (11, 13, 15) times, then every sixth row 8 (4, 3, 2) times—63 (67, 71, 73) sts. Cont even until sleeve measures 19 (19, 19½, 20)"/48.5 (48.5, 49.5, 51) cm from beg.

Shape Cap: Work same as back armhole shaping. BO rem 53 (57, 61, 63) sts.

Finishing

Sew shoulder seams.

Neckband: With RS facing, circular knitting needle, and B, pick up and K66 (66, 70, 70) around neckline, including sts from neck holders. Work K1 P1 rib for 1"/2.5 cm. Next Rnd: Change to A, and rib one rnd. BO **loosely** in rib.

Set in sleeves. Sew sleeve and side seams.

Girl's Swing Coat

Girl's Swing Coat

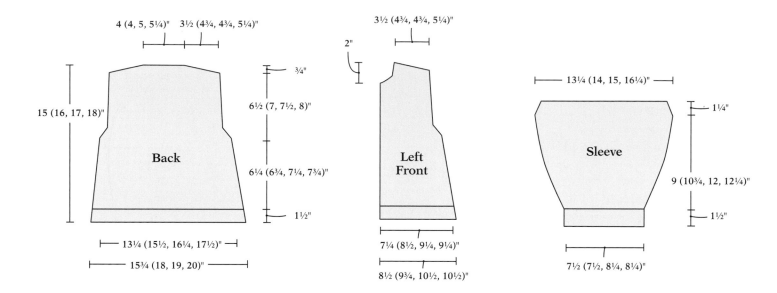

Skill Level
Beginner

Sizes
Child's size 2 (4, 6, 8). Instructions are for smallest size with changes for other sizes noted in parentheses as necessary.

Finished Measurements
Chest (Buttoned): 26¼ (31, 33¼, 34½)"/66.5 (78.5, 84.5, 87.5) cm
Length: 15 (16, 17, 18)"/38 (40.5, 43, 45.5) cm
Sleeve width at upper arm: 13¼ (14, 15, 16¼)"/33.5 (35.5, 38, 41) cm

Materials
- Muench's *Naturwolle* (bulky weight; 100% wool; 3½ oz/100 g; approx 110 yds/100 m), 5 (5, 6, 6) hanks Regenbogen #61

- Knitting needles, size 10½ (6.5 mm) or size needed to obtain gauge
- 16"/40 cm circular knitting needle, sizes 9 and 10 (5.5 and 6 mm)
- One stitch holder
- Three ⅞"/22 mm buttons (JHB International's *Peoria* style #45166 in Yellow was used on sample garment)

Gauge
In Stockinette St, 13 sts and 18 rows = 4"/10 cm. **To save time, take time to check gauge.**

Note
Instructions include 1 selvage st each side; these sts are not reflected in finished measurements.

Seed St
Same as for Woman's Shawl-Collar Cardigan.

Back
CO 53 (61, 63, 67) sts. Work Seed St until piece measures 1½"/4 cm from beg. Beg Stockinette St, and dec 1 st each side every fourth row 2 (0, 0, 0) times, then every sixth row 2 (4, 3, 2) times, then every eighth row 0 (0, 1, 2) times—45 (53, 55, 59) sts rem. Cont even until piece measures 7¾ (8¼, 8¾, 9¼)"/19.5 (21, 22, 23.5) cm from beg.

Shape Armholes: Dec 1 st each side every row twice, then dec 1 st each side every other row twice—37 (45, 47, 51) sts rem. Cont even until piece measures 14¼ (15¼, 16¼, 17¼)"/36 (38½, 41½, 44) cm from beg.

Shape Shoulders: BO 6 (8, 8, 8) sts at beg of next two rows, then BO 6 (8, 8, 9) sts at beg of next two rows. Slip rem 13 (13, 15, 17) sts onto holder for back of neck.

Left Front

CO 29 (33, 35, 35) sts. Work Seed St until piece measures 1½"/4 cm from beg. Next Row (RS): K24 (28, 30, 30), cont in Seed St to end row. Cont in Stockinette St with Seed St over 5 front band sts, and dec 1 st at armhole edge every fourth row 2 (0, 0, 0) times, then every sixth row 2 (4, 3, 2) times, then every eighth row 0 (0, 1, 2) times—25 (29, 31, 31) sts rem. Cont even in patt as established until piece measures 7¾ (8¼, 8¾, 9¼)"/19.5 (21, 22, 23.5) cm from beg, ending after WS row.

Shape Armhole: Dec 1 st at armhole edge every row twice, then every other row twice— 21 (25, 27, 27) sts rem. Cont even in patt as established until piece measures 13 (14, 15, 16)"/33 (35.5, 38, 40.5) cm from beg, ending after RS row.

Shape Neck: BO 5 sts at beg of next row, then BO 2 (2, 3, 3) sts at neck edge once, then dec 1 st at neck edge every row 2 (2, 3, 2) times; **and at the same time,** when piece measures same as back to shoulders, **Shape Shoulders** same as for back.
Place markers for three evenly spaced buttons, making the first ½" below neck shaping and the last 4"/10 cm below neck shaping.

Right Front

Work same as left front, *except* reverse all shaping and work 2-st buttonholes opposite markers on RS rows by working across RS rows until 4 sts rem, BO 2 sts, work to end row. On next row, cont in patt as established and CO 2 sts over the bound-off sts of previous row.

Sleeves

CO 25 (25, 27, 27) sts. Work Seed St until piece measures 1½"/4 cm from beg. Beg Stockinette St, and inc 1 st each side every other row 1 (0, 0, 2) times, every fourth row 9 (10, 11, 12) times, then every sixth row 0 (1, 1, 0) times—45 (47, 51, 55) sts. Cont even until sleeve measures 10½ (12¼, 13½, 13¾)"/26.5 (31, 34.5, 35) cm from beg.

Shape Cap: Work same as back armhole shaping. BO rem 37 (39, 43, 47) sts.

Finishing

Sew shoulder seams.
Collar: With RS facing and smaller circular knitting needle, pick up and K33 (33, 35, 37) around neckline including sts from back neck holder, beg and end halfway into front bands. Work Seed St for 1½"/4 cm. Next Row: Change to larger circular knitting needle, cont in Seed St, and inc 1 st at beg and end of row. Work even until collar measures 2¼"/5.5 cm from beg. Next Row: Cont in Seed St, and inc 1 st at beg and end of row. Work even until collar measures 3"/7.5 cm from beg. BO in Seed St.
Set in sleeves. Sew sleeve and side seams. Sew on buttons.

Seaside
Stripes

*Crisp nautical tones in lustrous mercerized cotton
are summer must-haves. Here, although the easy
slip stitch pattern is the same for all three sweaters,
notice how the different striping sequences yield
widely varied results.*

Woman's Sleeveless Pullover

Designer Hint

Be careful not to strand the yarn too tightly when slipping the stitches in Rows 1 and 3 of the Textured Patt. Use an even tension to keep the fabric uniform and to allow it to drape beautifully.

Skill Level
Intermediate

Sizes
Woman's Small (Medium, Large, Extra-Large). Instructions are for smallest size, with changes for other sizes noted in parentheses as necessary.

Finished Measurements
Bust: 34 (37, 40, 43)"/86.5 (94, 101.5, 109) cm
Length: 20 (21, 22, 23)"/51 (53.5, 56, 58.5) cm

Materials
* Classic Elite's *Provence* (sport weight; 100% mercerized cotton; 4½ oz/125 g; approx 256 yds/233 m), 1 (2, 2, 2) hank De Niemes Blue #2657 (**A**); 1 hank White #2601 (**B**); and 1 (2, 2, 2) hank Midnight Blue #2693 (**C**)
* Knitting needles, size 5 (4 mm) or size needed to obtain gauge
* Crochet hook, size F/5 (4 mm)
* One ⅜"/10 mm button (JHB International's *Moonstone* style #71622 in White was used on sample garment)

Gauge
In Textured Patt, 22 sts and 38 rows = 4"/10 cm. **To save time, take time to check gauge.**

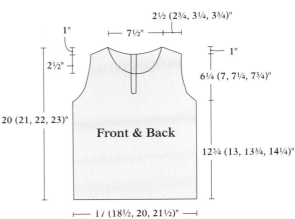

2½ (2¾, 3¼, 3¾)"

1" ⊢ 7½" ⊣

1"

2½"

6¼ (7, 7¼, 7¾)"

20 (21, 22, 23)"

Front & Back

12¾ (13, 13¾, 14¼)"

⊢ 17 (18½, 20, 21½)" ⊣

Textured Patt (multiple of 2 sts plus 1 st)

Row 1 (RS): K1, *slip next st with yarn in front, K1. Repeat from * across.

Row 2: Purl across.

Row 3: K2, *slip next st with yarn in front, K1. Repeat from * across, ending row with K1.

Row 4: Purl across.

Repeat Rows 1–4 in Color Sequence for patt.

Color Sequence

*14 rows A, 4 rows B, 14 rows C, 4 rows B. Repeat from * for patt.

Back

With A, CO 95 (103, 111, 119) sts. Work Textured Patt in Color Sequence until piece measures 12¾ (13, 13¾, 14¼)"/32.5 (33, 35, 36) cm from beg.

Shape Armholes: BO 5 (7, 8, 8) sts at beg of next two rows, then dec 1 st each side every other row 4 (4, 5, 5)

times, then every fourth row 4 (4, 4, 5) times—69 (73, 77, 83) sts rem. Cont even until all armhole decreases have been completed.

Divide for Neck Opening: Work across first 33 (35, 37, 40) sts, BO middle 3 sts; join second ball of yarn and work to end row. Work even on both sides at once with separate balls of yarn until armholes measure 6¼ (7, 7¼, 7¾)"/16 (18, 18.5, 19.5) cm.

Shape Neck and Shoulders: BO 3 (4, 4, 5) sts at beg of next six rows, then BO 4 (3, 5, 5) sts at beg of next two rows; **and at the same time,** BO 17 sts each neck edge once, then dec 1 st each neck edge every row three times.

Front

Work same as for back until armholes measure 3¾ (4½, 4¾, 5½)"/9.5 (11.5, 12, 13.3) cm, *except* do not divide for neck shaping.

Shape Neck: Work across first 25 (27,

29, 32) sts, BO middle 19 sts; join second ball of yarn and work to end row. Work both sides at once with separate balls of yarn, and BO 3 sts each neck edge once, BO 2 sts each neck edge twice, then dec 1 st each neck edge every other row five times. Cont even until piece measures same as back to shoulders.

Shape Shoulders: Same as for back.

Finishing

Sew shoulder seams. Sew side seams.

Armhole and Lower Edges: With RS facing, crochet hook, and B, work two rnds sc around armhole and lower edges. End off.

Neckband: Work same as armhole and lower edges, making ch2 button loop at top left edge of neck opening. Sew button onto right edge.

Man's Crew-Neck Pullover

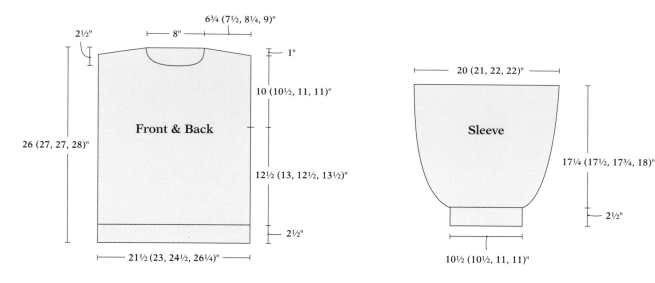

Skill Level
Advanced Beginner

Sizes
Man's Small (Medium, Large, Extra-Large). Instructions are for smallest size, with changes for other sizes noted in parentheses as necessary.

Finished Measurements
Chest: 43 (46, 49, 52½)"/109 (117, 124.5, 133.5) cm
Length: 26 (27, 27, 28)"/66 (68.5, 68.5, 71) cm
Sleeve width at upper arm: 20 (21, 22, 22)"/51 (53.5, 56, 56) cm

Materials
♦ Classic Elite's *Provence* (sport weight; 100% mercerized cotton; 4½ oz/125 g; approx 256 yds/233 m), 2 (2, 3, 3) hanks Midnight Blue #2693 (**A**); 4 (4, 5, 5) hanks White #2601 (**B**); and 2 (2, 3, 3) hanks De Niemes Blue #2657 (**C**)
♦ Knitting needles, sizes 4 and 5 (3.5 and 4 mm) or size needed to obtain gauge
♦ 16"/40 cm circular knitting needle, size 4 (3.5 mm)
♦ Two stitch holders

Gauge
With larger needles in Textured Patt, 22 sts and 38 rows = 4"/10 cm. **To save time, take time to check gauge.**

Textured Patt
Same as for Woman's Sleeveless Pullover.

Color Sequence
*2 rows A, 2 rows C, 4 rows B. Repeat from * for patt.

Back
With smaller needles and A, CO 119 (127, 135, 145) sts. Change to B and work K1 P1 rib for 2½"/6.5 cm. Next Row (WS): Change to larger needles, and purl across. Work Textured Patt in Color Sequence until piece measures 25 (26, 26, 27)"/63.5 (66, 66, 68.5) cm from beg.

Shape Shoulders: BO 7 (9, 9, 10) sts at beg of next six rows, then BO 8 (7, 9, 10) sts at beg of next four rows. Slip rem 45 sts onto holder for back of neck.

Front
Work same as back until piece measures 23½ (24½, 24½, 25½)" /59.5 (62, 62, 65) cm from beg.

Shape Neck: Work across first 50 (54, 58, 63) sts, slip middle 19 sts onto holder for front of neck; join second ball of yarn and work to end of row. Work both sides at once with separate balls of yarn, and BO 4 sts each neck edge once, BO 3 sts each neck edge once, BO 2 sts each neck edge once, then dec 1 st each neck edge every other row four times; **and at the same time,** when front measures same as back to shoulders, **Shape Shoulders** same as for back.

Sleeves

With smaller needles and A, CO 59 (59, 61, 61) sts. Change to B and work K1 P1 rib for 2½"/6.5 cm. Next Row (WS): Change to larger needles and purl across. Work Textured Patt in Color Sequence, and inc 1 st each side every fourth row 2 (6, 11, 10) times, then every sixth row 24 (22, 19, 20) times— 111 (115, 121, 121) sts. Cont even until sleeve measures 19¾ (20, 20¼, 20½)"/50 (51, 51.5, 52) cm from the beg. BO.

Finishing

Sew shoulder seams.

Neckband: With RS facing, circular knitting needle, and B, pick up and K102 around neckline, including sts from neck holders. Work rnds of K1 P1 rib for 1"/2.5 cm. Change to A and BO in rib.

Place markers 10 (10½, 11, 11)"/25.5 (26.5, 28, 28) cm down from shoulders. Set in sleeves between markers. Sew sleeve and side seams.

Infant's Pullover

Skill Level
Intermediate

Sizes
Infant's 6 (12, 18) months. Instructions are written for smallest size, with changes for other sizes noted in parentheses as necessary.

Finished Measurements
Chest: 22 (24, 26)"/56 (61, 66) cm
Length: 11 (12, 13)"/28 (30.5, 33) cm
Sleeve width at upper arm: 9½ (10, 10½)"/24 (25.5, 26.5) cm

Materials
- Classic Elite's *Provence* (sport weight; 100% mercerized cotton; 4½ oz/125 g; approx 256 yds/233 m), 1 (2, 2) hank White #2601 (**A**) and 1 hank each of De Niemes Blue #2657 (**B**) and Midnight Blue #2693 (**C**)
- Knitting needles, sizes 4 and 5 (3.5 and 4 mm) or size needed to obtain gauge
- 16"/40 cm circular knitting needle, size 4 (3.5 mm)
- Two stitch holders
- Four ½"/15 mm buttons (JHB International's *Moonstone* style #71623 in White was used in sample garment)

Gauge
With larger needles in Textured Patt, 22 sts and 38 rows = 4"/10 cm. **To save time, take time to check gauge.**

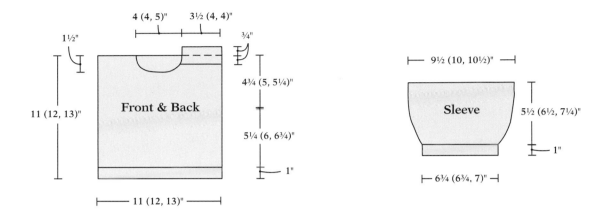

Textured Patt
Same as for Woman's Sleeveless Pullover.

Color Sequence
One row each of *A, B, C. Repeat from * for patt.

Back
With smaller needles and A, CO 61 (67, 71) sts. Work K1 P1 rib for 1"/2.5 cm. Next Row (WS): Change to larger needles and C, and purl across. Work Textured Patt in Color Sequence until piece measures 11 (12, 13)"/28 (30.5, 33) cm from beg, ending after WS row. BO 42 (45, 49) sts. Slip rem 19 (22, 22) sts onto holder for button band.

Front
Work same as back until piece measures 9½ (10½, 11½)"/24 (26.5, 29) cm from beg, ending after WS row.
Shape Neck: Work across first 24 (27, 28) sts, slip middle 13 (13, 15) sts onto holder for front of neck; join second ball of yarn and work to end row.

Work both sides at once with separate balls of yarn, and BO 3 (3, 4) sts each neck edge once, then BO 2 sts each neck edge once. Next Row (WS): Work across right shoulder sts, slip 19 (22, 22) left shoulder sts onto holder for buttonhole band. Work even on right shoulder sts until front measures same as back. BO.

Sleeves
With smaller needles and A, CO 37 (37, 39) sts. Work K1 P1 rib for 1"/2.5 cm. Next Row (WS): Change to larger needles and C, and purl across. Beg Textured Patt in Color Sequence, and inc 1 st each side every fourth row 3 (2, 0) times, then every sixth row 5 (7, 9) times—53 (55, 57) sts. Cont even until sleeve measures 6½ (7½, 8¼)"/16.5 (19, 21) cm from beg. BO.

Finishing
Sew right shoulder seam.
Neckband: With circular knitting needle and A, pick up and K55 (55, 59) around neckline, including sts from front neck holder. Work K1 P1 Rib for 1"/2.5 cm. BO in rib.
Button Band: With RS facing, smaller needles, and A, pick up and K6 along side of neckband, then K19 (22, 22) from button band holder—25 (28, 28) sts total. Work K1 P1 rib for 1"/2.5 cm. BO in rib. Place markers for four evenly spaced buttons along button band.
Buttonhole Band: With RS facing, smaller needles, and A, pick up and K19 (22, 22) from right shoulder holder, then pick up and K6 along side of neckband—25 (28, 28) sts total. Work K1 P1 rib for ½"/1.5 cm. Next Row: Make buttonholes opposite markers by working (k2tog, yarn over). Cont until band measures 1"/2.5 cm. BO in rib. Overlap buttonhole band over button band and sew armhole ends tog.
Place markers 4¾ (5, 5¼)"/12 (12.5, 13.5) cm down from shoulders. Set in sleeves between markers. Sew sleeve and side seams. Sew on buttons.

Nordic
Warmth

These fun-to-knit sweaters are great for late fall and winter family outings. Look closely, and you will see that the adult sweaters are worked from identical Fair Isle charts with their colors reversed.

Woman's Zippered High-Neck

Designer Hint

Would you like to save a step when setting in sleeves for dropped-shoulder sweaters? Rather than bind off the sleeve stitches, use a crochet hook and slip stitch those live stitches directly into the armhole. As an extra bonus, the seam will be less bulky.

Skill Level
Intermediate

Sizes
Woman's Small (Medium, Large). Instructions are for smallest size, with changes for other sizes noted in parentheses as necessary.

Finished Measurements
Bust: 41½ (44½, 47½)"/105.5 (113, 120.5) cm
Length: 22 (22, 23)"/56 (56, 58.5) cm
Sleeve width at upper arm: 17 (18, 19)"/43 (45.5, 48.5) cm

Materials
- JCA/Reynolds's *Candide* (heavy worsted weight; 100% wool; 3½ oz/100 g; approx 170 yds/155 m), 4 (4, 5) hanks Navy #4 (**A**) and 3 (4, 4) hanks Washed White #6 (**B**)
- Knitting needles, sizes 9 and 10 (5.5 and 6.5 mm) or size needed to obtain gauge
- 16"/40 cm circular knitting needle, size 9 (5.5 mm)
- One stitch holder
- One safety pin
- 7"/18 cm zipper

Gauge
With larger needles in Woman's Main Fair Isle Patt, 16 sts and 18 rows = 4"/10 cm. **To save time, take time to check gauge.**

Back
With larger needles and A, CO 85 (91, 97) sts. Work K1 P1 rib for 1½"/4 cm. Next Row (WS): Purl across. Beg and end where indicated, work Rows 1 to 6 of Woman's Border Patt. Beg and end where indicated, repeat Rows 1 to 24 of Woman's Main Fair Isle Patt until piece measures 12 (11½, 12)"/30.5 (29, 30.5) cm from beg.
Shape Armholes: BO 6 sts at beg of next two rows—73 (79, 85) sts rem. Cont even in patt until armholes measure 8½ (9, 9½)"/21.5 (23, 24) cm.
Shape Shoulders: BO 8 (9, 10) sts at beg of next four rows, then BO 7 (8, 9) sts at beg of next two rows. Slip rem 27 sts onto holder for back of neck.

Front
Work same as back until armholes measure 3½ (4, 4½)"/9 (10, 11.5) cm.
Divide for Zipper Opening: Work across first 35 (38, 41) sts, slip middle 3 sts onto safety pin; join second ball of yarn and work to end of row. Work both sides at once with separate balls of yarn until armholes measure 7½ (8, 8½)"/19 (20.5, 21.5) cm.
Shape Neck: BO 4 sts each neck edge once, BO 3 sts each neck edge twice, then dec 1 st each neck edge every row twice; **and at the same time,** when front measures same as back to shoulders, **Shape Shoulders** same as for back.

Sleeves
With larger needles and A, CO 39 sts. Work K1 P1 rib for 1½"/4 cm. Next Row (WS): Purl across, inc 4 sts evenly across—43 sts. Beg and end Woman's Border Patt where indicated. Inc 1 st each side on next row and again on Row 6 of chart. Beg and end Woman's Main Fair Isle Patt where indicated,

Woman's Zippered High-Neck

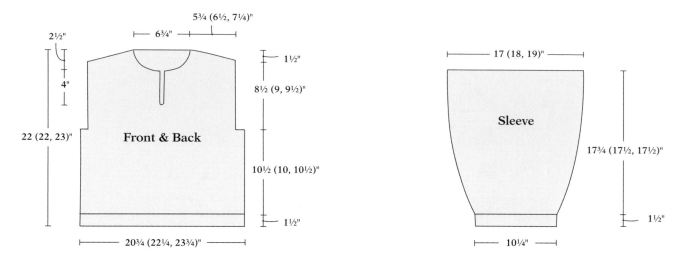

and inc 1 st each side every fourth row 3 (10, 15) times, then every sixth row 8 (3, 0) times—69 (73, 77) sts. Work even until sleeve measures 19¼ (19, 19)"/49 (48.5, 48.5) cm from beg. BO.

Finishing

Sew shoulder seams.

Neckband: With RS facing, circular knitting needle, and A, pick up and K59 around neckline, including sts from back neck holder. Work back and forth in rows of K1 P1 rib for 3"/7.5 cm. BO in rib.

Zipper Facing: With RS facing, smaller needles, and A, pick up and K33 along left side of center front opening, pick up and K3 from safety pin, pick up and K33 along right side of center front opening—69 sts. Next Row: Knit to BO. Sew in zipper. Set in sleeves. Sew sleeve and side seams.

Woman's Main Fair Isle Patt

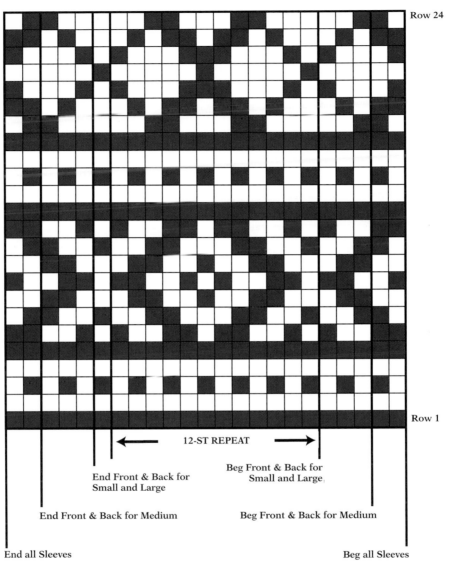

Row 24

Row 1

← 12-ST REPEAT →

End Front & Back for
Small and Large

Beg Front & Back for
Small and Large

End Front & Back for Medium

Beg Front & Back for Medium

End all Sleeves

Beg all Sleeves

Key

 = A

☐ = B

Woman's Border Patt

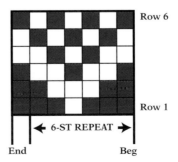

Row 6

Row 1

← 6-ST REPEAT →

End

Beg

Man's Turtleneck

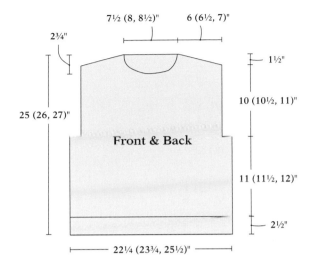

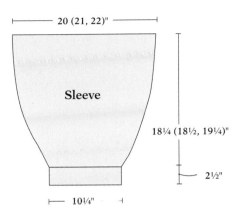

Sizes

Man's Small (Medium, Large).
Instructions are for smallest size, with
changes for other sizes noted in
parentheses as necessary.

Finished Measurements

Chest: 44½ (47½, 51)"/113 (120.5,
129.5) cm
Length: 25 (26, 27)"/63.5 (66, 68.5) cm
Sleeve width at upper arm: 20 (21,
22)"/51 (53.5, 56) cm

Materials

- JCA/Reynolds's *Candide* (heavy
  worsted weight; 100% wool;
  3½ oz/100 g; approx 170 yds/155 m),
  5 (5, 6) hanks Washed White #6 (**A**)
  and 4 (4, 5) hanks Navy #4 (**B**)
- Knitting needles, sizes 8 and 10 (5
  and 6.5 mm) or size needed to
  obtain gauge
- 16"/40 cm circular knitting needle,
  size 8 (5 mm)
- Two stitch holders

Gauge

With larger needles in Man's Fair Isle
Patt, 16 sts and 18 rows = 4"/10 cm. **To
save time, take time to check gauge.**

Back

With smaller needles and B, CO 91 (97,
103) sts. Change to A, and work K1 P1
rib for 2½"/6.5 cm. Next Row (WS):
Purl across. Beg and end where
indicated, work Rows 1 to 6 of Man's
Border Patt. Beg and end where
indicated, repeat Rows 1 to 24 of
Man's Main Fair Isle Patt until piece
measures 13½ (14, 14½)"/34.5 (35.5,
37) cm from beg.
Shape Armholes: BO 6 sts at beg of
next two rows—79 (85, 91) sts rem.
Cont even in patt until armholes
measure 10 (10½, 11)"/25.5 (26.5,
28) cm.

Shape Shoulders: BO 8 (9, 9) sts at
beg of next four rows, then BO 8 (8,
10) sts at beg of next two rows. Slip
rem 31 (33, 35) sts onto holder for
back of neck.

Front

Work same as back until armholes
measure 8¾ (9¼, 9¾)"/22 (23.5,
25) cm.
Shape Neck: Work across first 32 (35,
38) sts, slip middle 15 sts onto holder
for front of neck; join second ball of
yarn and work to end row. Work both
sides at once with separate balls of
yarn, and BO 3 (4, 4) sts each neck
edge once, BO 2 sts each neck edge
twice, then dec 1 st each neck edge
every row once (once, twice); **and at
the same time,** when front measures
same as back to shoulders, **Shape
Shoulders** same as for back.

Sleeves

With smaller needles and B, CO 39 sts. Change to A, and work K1 P1 rib for 2½"/6.5 cm. Next Row (WS): Purl across, inc 4 sts evenly across—43 sts. Beg and end Man's Border Patt where indicated. Inc 1 st each side on next row and on Rows 4 and 6 of chart. Beg and end Man's Main Fair Isle Patt where indicated, and inc 1 st each side every other row 0 (3, 6) times, then every fourth row 16 (15, 14) times—81 (85, 89) sts. Work even until sleeve measures 20¾ (21, 21¾)"/52.5 (53.5, 55) cm from beg. BO.

Finishing

Sew shoulder seams.

Neckband: With RS facing, circular knitting needle, and A, pick up and K74 (78, 82) around neckline, including sts from neck holders. Work K1 P1 rib for 6"/15 cm. Change to B, and BO in rib.

Set in sleeves. Sew sleeve and side seams.

Man's Main Fair Isle Patt

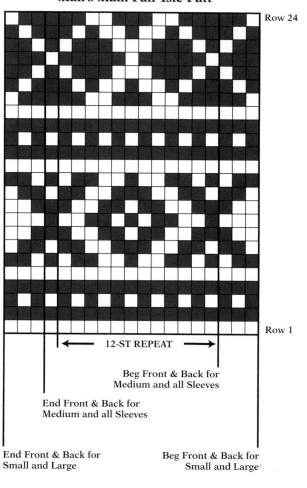

Row 24

Row 1

◄——— 12-ST REPEAT ———►

Beg Front & Back for
Medium and all Sleeves

End Front & Back for
Medium and all Sleeves

End Front & Back for
Small and Large

Beg Front & Back for
Small and Large

Key

☐ = A
■ = B

Man's Border Patt

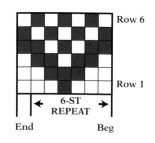

Row 6

Row 1

◄ 6-ST ►
REPEAT

End   Beg

Child's Crew-Neck Pullover

Skill Level
Intermediate

Sizes
Child's size 2 (4, 6, 8). Instructions are for smallest size, with changes for other sizes noted in parentheses as necessary.

Finished Measurements
Chest: 27 (30, 33, 36)"/68.5 (76, 84, 91.5) cm
Length: 14 (16, 18, 19)"/35.5 (40.5, 45.5, 48.5) cm
Sleeve width at upper arm: 12 (13, 14, 15)"/30.5 (33, 35.5, 38) cm

Materials
* JCA/Reynolds's *Candide* (heavy worsted weight; 100% wool; 3½ oz/100 g; approx 170 yds/155 m), 3 (3, 4, 4) hanks Navy #4 (**A**) and 1 (1, 1, 2) hank Washed White #6 (**B**)
* Knitting needles, sizes 9 and 10 (5.5 and 6.5 mm) or size needed to obtain gauge
* 16"/40 cm circular knitting needle, sizes 9 and 10 (5.5 and 6.5 mm) or size needed to obtain gauge
* Two stitch holders

Gauge
With larger needles in Child's Main Fair Isle Patt, 16 sts and 18 rows = 4"/10 cm. **To save time, take time to check gauge.**

Back
With smaller needles and B, CO 55 (61, 67, 73) sts. Change to A, and work K1 P1 rib for 1"/2.5 cm. Next Row (WS): Purl across. Change to larger needles, beg and end where indicated, and

work Rows 1 to 22 of Child's Border Patt. Beg and end where indicated, repeat Rows 1 to 6 of Child's Main Fair Isle Patt until piece measures 12½ (14½, 16½, 17½)"/31.5 (37, 42, 44.5) cm from beg.

Shape Neck and Shoulders: Work across first 15 (17, 19, 21) sts, slip middle 25 (27, 29, 31) sts onto holder for front of neck; join second ball of yarn and work to end of row. Work both sides at once with separate balls of yarn, and dec 1 st each neck edge every other row three times; **and at the same time,** when back measures 13¼ (15¼, 17¼, 18¼)"/33.5 (38.5, 44, 46.5) cm from beg, BO 6 (7, 8, 9) sts each shoulder edge twice.

Front
Work same as back until piece measures 11¼ (13¼, 14¾, 15¾)"/28.5 (33.5, 37.5, 40) cm from beg.

Shape Neck: Work across first 21 (23, 26, 28) sts, slip middle 13 (15, 15, 17) sts onto holder for front of neck; join second ball of yarn and work to end row. Work both sides at once with separate balls of yarn, and BO 3 sts each neck edge twice, 2 sts each neck edge once, then dec 1 st each neck edge every row once (once, twice, twice); **and at the same time,** when front measures same as back to shoulders, **Shape Shoulders** same as for back.

Sleeves
With smaller needles and B, CO 27 (27, 33, 33) sts. Change to A, and work K1 P1 rib for 1"/2.5 cm. Next Row (WS): Purl across. Change to larger needles, beg and end where indicated, and

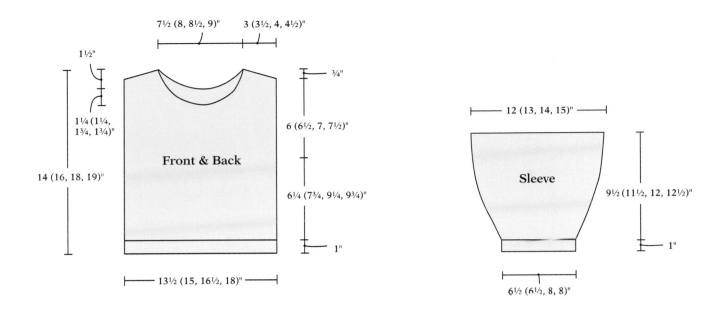

Front & Back

7½ (8, 8½, 9)" 3 (3½, 4, 4½)"

1½"

1¼ (1¼, 1¾, 1¾)"

14 (16, 18, 19)"

¾"

6 (6½, 7, 7½)"

6¼ (7¾, 9¼, 9¾)"

1"

13½ (15, 16½, 18)"

Sleeve

12 (13, 14, 15)"

9½ (11½, 12, 12½)"

1"

6½ (6½, 8, 8)"

work Rows 1 to 22 of Child's Border Patt; then beg and end where indicated, and repeat Rows 1 to 6 of Child's Main Fair Isle Patt; **and at the same time,** inc 1 st each side every other row 3 (5, 0, 1) times, then every fourth row 8 (8, 12, 13) times—49 (53, 57, 61) sts. Work even until sleeve measures 10½ (12½, 13, 13½)"/26.5 (32, 33, 34.5) cm from beg. BO.

Finishing

Sew shoulder seams.

Neckband: With RS facing, larger circular knitting needle, and A, pick up and K72 (76, 80, 84) around neckline, including sts from neck holders. Work Rows 8 to 10 of Child's Border Patt once, dec 8 sts evenly on last rnd— 64 (68, 72, 76) sts. Change to smaller circular knitting needle, cont with A, and work K1 P1 rib for 1"/2.5 cm. Change to B, and BO in rib.

Place markers 6 (6½, 7, 7½)"/15 (16.5, 18, 19) cm down from shoulders. Set in sleeves between markers. Sew sleeve and side seams.

Child's Border Patt

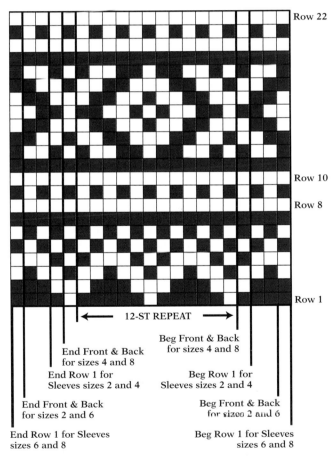

Row 22

Row 10

Row 8

Row 1

12-ST REPEAT

End Front & Back for sizes 4 and 8
End Row 1 for Sleeves sizes 2 and 4
End Front & Back for sizes 2 and 6
End Row 1 for Sleeves sizes 6 and 8

Beg Front & Back for sizes 4 and 8
Beg Row 1 for Sleeves sizes 2 and 4
Beg Front & Back for sizes 2 and 6
Beg Row 1 for Sleeves sizes 6 and 8

Child's Main Fair Isle Patt

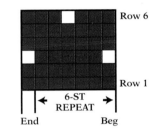

Row 6

Row 1

6-ST REPEAT

End   Beg

Key

■ = A
□ = B

The South Hadley Tweeds

Rich harvest colors in a wonderful flecked yarn make this his and hers cardigan duo perfect for crisp autumn days. Changing the placement of the cable panels from his sleeves to her torso shifts the focus from his broad saddle shoulders to her shaped silhouette.

Woman's Shaped Cardigan

Skill Level
Expert

Sizes
Woman's Small (Medium, Large). Instructions are for smallest size, with changes for other sizes noted in parentheses as necessary.

Finished Measurements
Bust (Buttoned): 39¼ (42¾, 46¼)"/99.5 (108.5, 117.5) cm
Waist: 34¾ (38½, 41¼)"/88 (97.5, 104.5) cm
Hip: 42¼ (45¾, 48¼)"/ 107 (116, 122.5) cm
Length: 27 (28, 29)"/68.5 (71, 73.5) cm
Sleeve width at upper arm: 15 (15½, 16)"/38 (39.5, 40.5) cm

Materials
- Tahki Import's *Donegal Tweed* (heavy worsted weight; 100% wool; 3½ oz/100 g; approx 183 yds/167 m), 8 (9, 10) hanks Butterscotch #802
- Knitting needles, sizes 7 and 8 (4.5 and 5 mm) or size needed to obtain gauge
- Two stitch holders
- Cable needle
- Ten 1"/25 mm buttons (JHB International's *Adventurer* style #92408 in Bronze was used on sample garment)

Designer Hint
To sew the pocket linings neatly to the WS, poke a double-pointed knitting needle through a straight column of stitches on the WS of the front. Row for row, whipstitch these stitches to the sides of the lining.

Gauge
With larger needles in Stockinette St, 18 sts and 24 rows = 4"/10 cm. **To save time, take time to check gauge.**

Back
With smaller needles, CO 98 (106, 112) sts. Work K1 P1 rib for 1"/2.5 cm, inc 24 sts evenly across last row—122 (130, 136) sts. Change to larger needles.
Establish Patt: Next Row (RS): Knit 11 (14, 16) sts, place marker, work Row 1 of South Hadley Tweed Cable Panel over next 36 sts, place marker, knit middle 28 (30, 32) sts, place marker, work Row 1 of South Hadley Tweed Cable Panel over next 36 sts, knit to end row. Cont in patt as established until piece measures 6 (6½, 7)"/15 (16.5, 18) cm from beg, ending after WS row.
Decrease for Waist: Dec 1 st each side every other row eight times—106 (114, 120) sts. Cont even until piece measures 10 (10½, 11)"/25.5 (26.5, 28) cm from beg.

Increase for Bust: Inc 1 st each side every other row five times—116 (124, 130) sts. Cont even until piece measures 17½ (18, 18½)"/44.5 (45.5, 47) cm from beg.
Shape Armholes: BO 2 (4, 5) sts at beg of next two rows, then dec 1 st each side every other row five times—102 (106, 110) sts rem. Cont even until armholes measure 8½ (9, 9½)"/21.5 (23, 24) cm.
Shape Shoulders: BO 13 (13, 14) sts at beg of next four rows, then BO 12 (14, 14) sts at beg of next two rows. Slip rem 26 sts onto holder for back of neck.

South Hadley Tweed Cable Panel

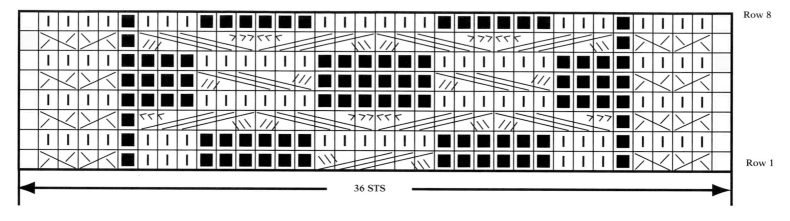

Row 8

Row 1

◄—————————————— 36 STS ——————————————►

Pocket Lining (Make Two)

With larger needles, CO 20 sts. Work Stockinette St for 4½"/11.5 cm, ending after RS row. Slip sts onto holder.

Left Front

With smaller needles, CO 59 (63, 67) sts. Row 1 (WS): P13, place marker, work K1 P1 rib to end row. Next Row: Work in rib as established to marker, K6, slip next st, K6 to end row. Repeat last two rows until piece measures 1"/2.5 cm from beg, ending after RS row. Next Row: P13, work rib as established to end row, inc 12 sts evenly across—71 (75, 79) sts. Change to larger needles.

Establish Patt: Next Row (RS): K11 (14, 16), place marker, work Row 1 of South Hadley Tweed Cable Panel over next 36 sts, place marker, knit to next marker, K6, slip next st, K6 to end row. Cont in patt as established until piece measures 5½"/14 cm from beg, ending after RS row. Note pattern row of cable panel.

Place Pocket Lining (WS): P24 (25, 27), slip next 36 sts onto holder, purl across sts from one pocket lining holder **increasing 16 sts evenly,** purl to end row. Next Row (RS): Cont in patt as established until piece measures 6 (6½, 7)"/15 (16.5, 18) cm from beg, ending after WS row.

Decrease for Waist (RS): Dec 1 st at beg of next row and every other row seven more times—63 (67, 71) sts rem. Cont even until piece measures 10 (10½, 11)"/25.5 (26.5, 28) cm from beg, ending after WS row.

Increase for Bust (RS): Inc 1 st at beg of next row and every other row four more times—68 (72, 76) sts. Cont even until piece measures 17½ (18, 18½)"/44.5 (45.5, 47) cm from beg, ending after WS row.

Woman's Shaped Cardigan

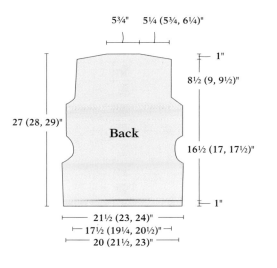

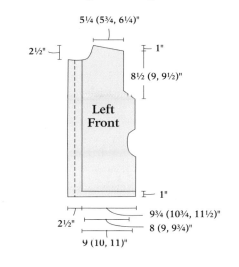

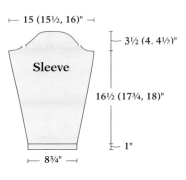

Shape Armhole (RS): BO 2 (4, 5) sts at beg of next row, then dec 1 st at armhole edge every other row five times—61 (63, 66) sts rem. Cont even until armhole measures 7 (7½, 8)"/18 (19, 20.5) cm, ending after RS row.

Shape Neck (WS): BO first 13 sts, work to end row. BO 4 sts at neck edge once, BO 3 sts at neck edge once, then dec 1 st at neck edge every row 3 (3, 4) times; **and at the same time,** when piece measures same as back to shoulders, **Shape Shoulder** same as for back.

Place markers for ten evenly spaced buttons along band, making the first and last ½"/1.5 cm from top and bottom edges of band.

Right Front

Work same as left front, *except* reverse all shaping and placement of patt, front band, and pocket. Work 10 buttonholes opposite markers on RS rows as follows: K1, BO next 4 sts, K1, slip next st, K1, BO next 4 sts, work to end of row. On next row, CO 4 sts over the bound-off sts from previous row.

Sleeves

With smaller needles, CO 40 sts. Work K1 P1 rib for 1"/2.5 cm. Change to larger needles, beg Stockinette St, and inc 1 st each side every sixth row 10 (10, 13) times, then every eighth row 4 (5, 3) times—68 (70, 72) sts. Work even until sleeve measures 17½ (18¾, 19)"/44.5 (47.5, 48.5) cm from beg.

Shape Cap: BO 2 (4, 5) sts at beg of next two rows, then dec 1 st each side every other row 0 (2, 6) times, then every row 12 (10, 6) times. BO 3 sts at beg of next four rows, then BO 4 sts at beg of next four rows. BO rem 12 (10, 10) sts.

Finishing

Sew shoulder seams. Fold and sew facing of front bands to WS.

Pocket Edgings: With RS facing and smaller needles, pick up and knit sts from pocket holder. Work K1 P1 rib for 1"/2.5 cm. BO in rib. Sew sides of pocket edge to front. Sew pocket linings to WS of front.

Sew on buttons. Work buttonhole st around buttonholes and along top and bottom edge of front bands.

Set in sleeves. Sew sleeve and side seams.

Collar: With RS facing and smaller needles, beg and end halfway across each front band, pick up and K75 around neckline, including sts from back neck holder. Work K1 P1 rib for 1½"/4 cm. Change to larger needles, and cont in rib as established for 1½"/4 cm more. BO in rib.

Man's Cardigan

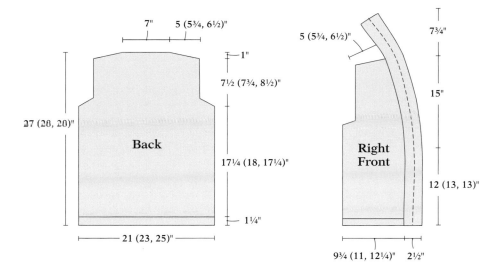

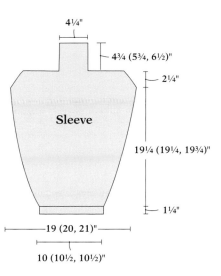

Skill Level
Intermediate

Sizes
Man's Small (Medium, Large). Instructions are for smallest size, with changes for other sizes noted in parentheses as necessary.

Finished Measurements
Chest (Buttoned): 42 (46, 50)"/106.5 (116.5, 127) cm
Length: 29¼ (30¼, 30¼)"/74.5 (77, 77) cm
Sleeve width at upper arm: 19 (20, 21)"/48.5 (51, 53.5) cm

Materials
- Tahki Import's *Donegal Tweed* (heavy worsted weight; 100% wool; 3½ oz/100 g; approx. 183 yds/167 m), 10 (10, 11) hanks Copper #893
- Knitting needles, sizes 7 and 8 (4.5 and 5 mm) or size needed to obtain gauge
- Two stitch holders
- Cable needle
- Five 1"/25 mm buttons (JHB International's *Don Quixote* style #82630 in Brown Pewter was used on sample garment)

Gauge
With larger needles in Stockinette St, 18 sts and 24 rows = 4"/10 cm. **To save time, take time to check gauge.**

Back
With smaller needles, CO 96 (104, 114) sts. Work K1 P1 rib for 1¼"/3 cm. Change to larger needles, and work Stockinette St until piece measures 18½ (19¼, 18½)"/47 (49, 47) cm from beg.
Shape Armholes: BO 4 (4, 5) sts at beg of next two rows, then dec 1 st each side every other row six times—76 (84, 92) sts rem. Work even until armholes measure 7½ (7¾, 8½)"/19 (19.5, 21.5) cm.
Shape Shoulders: BO 7 (9, 10) sts at beg of next four rows, then BO 8 (8, 10) sts at beg of next two rows. BO rem 32 sts for back of neck.

Pocket Lining (Make Two)
With larger needles, CO 26 sts. Work Stockinette St for 5½"/14 cm, ending after WS row. Slip sts onto holder.

Right Front
With smaller needles, CO 59 (63, 69) sts. Row 1 (RS): K6, slip next st, K6, place marker, *P1, K1. Repeat from * across to end row. Row 2: *P1, K1. Repeat from * to marker, then P13. Repeat last two rows until piece measures 1¼"/3 cm, ending after WS row. Change to larger needles. Next Row (RS): K6, slip next st, K6, slip marker, knit to end row. Next Row (WS): Purl. Repeat last two rows until piece measures 6¾"/17 cm from beg, ending after WS row.
Place Pocket Lining: Next Row (RS): K6, slip next st, K6, slip marker, K10 (12, 15), slip next 26 sts onto holder and with RS facing, K26 from one pocket lining, work in Stockinette St to end row. Cont in Stockinette St working front band as established

until piece measures 12 (13, 13)"/30.5 (33, 33) cm from beg, ending after WS row.

Shape Neck: Next Row (Decrease Row) (RS): Work across first 13 sts as established, ssk, work to end row. Cont in Stockinette St and repeat dec row every eighth row 3 more times, then every sixth row 10 times; **and at the same time,** when piece measures same as back to underarm, BO 4 (4, 6) sts at armhole edge, then dec 1 st at armhole edge every other row six times, and when piece measures same as back to shoulders, **Shape Shoulder** same as for back. Cont even on 13 band sts for 7¾"/19.5 cm more. BO. Place markers for five evenly spaced buttons along band, making the first at beg of neck shaping and the last ½"/1.5 cm from bottom edge.

Left Front

Work same as right front, *except* reverse all shaping, and work neck decreases as follows: Work to 2 sts before marker, k2tog, work to end row. Make five 4-st buttonholes opposite markers on RS rows as follows: work across to marker, K1, BO next 4 sts, K1, slip next st, K1, BO next 4 sts, K1. On next row, CO 4 sts over the bound-off sts from previous row.

Sleeves

With smaller needles, CO 50 (52, 52) sts. Work K1 P1 rib for 1¼"/3 cm, inc 12 sts evenly across last row—62 (64, 64) sts. Change to larger needles.

Establish Patt: Next Row (RS): K13 (14, 14), place marker, work Row 1 of South Hadley Tweed Cable Panel over middle 36 sts, place marker, knit to end row. Cont in Stockinette St with South Hadley Tweed Cable Panel over middle 36 sts, and inc 1 st each side every fourth row 5 (11, 15) times, then every sixth row 15 (11, 9) times—102 (108, 112) sts. Work even until sleeve measures 20½ (20½, 21)"/52 (52, 53.5) cm from beg.

Shape Cap: BO 4 (4, 5) sts at beg of next two rows, then dec 1 st each side every other row six times—82 (88, 90) sts rem. BO 23 (26, 27) sts at beg of next two rows—36 sts rem. Cont even on these sts for 4¾ (5¾, 6½)"/12 (14.5, 16.5) cm for saddle. BO.

Finishing

Sew back and front shoulders to saddle. Set in sleeve. Sew sleeve and side seams. Seam neckband, and sew to back of neck, folding facing to WS. Fold and sew facing of front bands to WS. Work buttonhole stitch around buttonholes and along bottom edge of bands.

Pocket Edging: With RS facing and smaller needles, pick up and knit sts from pocket holders. Work K1 P1 rib for 1"/2.5 cm. BO in rib. Sew sides of pocket edge to RS of front. Sew pocket linings to WS of front.
Sew on buttons.

Cabled Elegance

Abundant cable crossings and dimensional knit/purl stitches create the richly textured fabric in these three sweaters. Styling details, such as the man's cabled edging and the woman's side slits, add to their casual elegance.

Woman's Tunic

Skill Level
Intermediate

Sizes
Woman's Small (Medium, Large). Instructions are for smallest size, with changes for other sizes noted in parentheses as necessary.

Finished Measurements
Bust: 42 (45½, 49)"/106.5 (115.5, 124.5) cm
Length: 28 (29, 29)"/71 (73.5, 73.5) cm
Sleeve width at upper arm: 17 (18, 19)"/43 (45.5, 48.5) cm

Materials
- Unique Kolours/Cynthia Helene's *Merino DK 8-ply* (sport weight; 100% wool; 1¾ oz/50 g; approx 123 yds/113 m), 23 (24, 25) balls Currant #270
- Knitting needles, sizes 4 and 6 (3.5 and 4 mm) or size needed to obtain gauge
- 16"/40 cm circular knitting needle, size 4 (3.5 mm)
- Cable needle

Gauge
With larger needles in Cable Patt, 36 sts and 32 rows = 4"/10 cm. **To save time, take time to check gauge.**

Seed St
Row 1 (RS): *K1, P1. Repeat from * across, ending row with K1.
Row 2: Knit the purl sts and purl the knit sts.
Repeat Rows 1 and 2 for patt.

Back
With smaller needles, CO 132 (142, 152) sts. Work Seed St for eleven rows. Next Row (WS): Cont in Seed St, work across first 7 sts, place marker, inc 58 (64, 70) sts evenly across next 118 (128, 138) sts, place marker, work to end of row—190 (206, 222) sts. Change to larger needles. Work Rows 1 to 24 of Woman's Border Patt, then repeat Rows 1 to 24 of Cable Patt until piece measures 27 (28, 28)"/68.5 (71, 71) cm from beg.
Shape Shoulders: BO 16 (17, 19) sts at beg of next six rows, then BO 16 (18, 19) sts at beg of next two rows. BO rem 62 (68, 70) sts for back of neck.

Front
Work same as back until piece measures 25½ (26½, 26½)"/65 (67.5, 67.5) cm from beg.
Shape Neck: Work across first 83 (90, 97) sts; join second ball of yarn and BO middle 24 (26, 28) sts, work to end row. Work both sides at once with

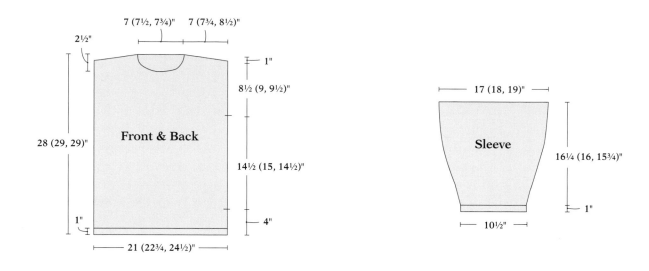

separate balls of yarn, and BO 6 sts each neck edge once, BO 4 sts each neck edge once, BO 2 sts each neck edge 3 (4, 4) times, then dec 1 st each neck edge every row three times; **and at the same time,** when front measures same as back to shoulder, **Shape Shoulders** same as for back.

Sleeves

With smaller needles, CO 64 sts. Work Seed St for eleven rows. Next Row (WS): Cont in Seed St, and inc 30 sts evenly across—94 sts. Change to larger needles. Beg Cable Patt, repeat Rows 1 to 24, and inc 1 st each side every other row 0 (7, 18) times, then every fourth row 30 (27, 21) times—154 (162, 172) sts. Work even until sleeve measures 17¼ (17, 16¾)"/44 (43, 42.5) cm from beg. BO.

Finishing

Sew shoulder seams.
Neckband: With RS facing and circular knitting needle, pick up and knit 102 (106, 108) sts around neck-line. Work rnds of Seed St for ½"/1.5 cm. Next Rnd: Cont in Seed St, working double decrease at each shoulder by working (k2tog, p2tog)—98 (102, 104) sts rem. Cont even until band measures 1"/2.5 cm from beg. Next Rnd: Cont in Seed St, working double decreases at shoulders as before—94 (98, 100) sts rem. BO. Place markers 8½ (9, 9½)"/21.5 (23, 24) cm down from shoulders. Set in sleeves between markers. Sew sleeve and side seams, leaving bottom 4"/10 cm open for side slits.

Cable Patt

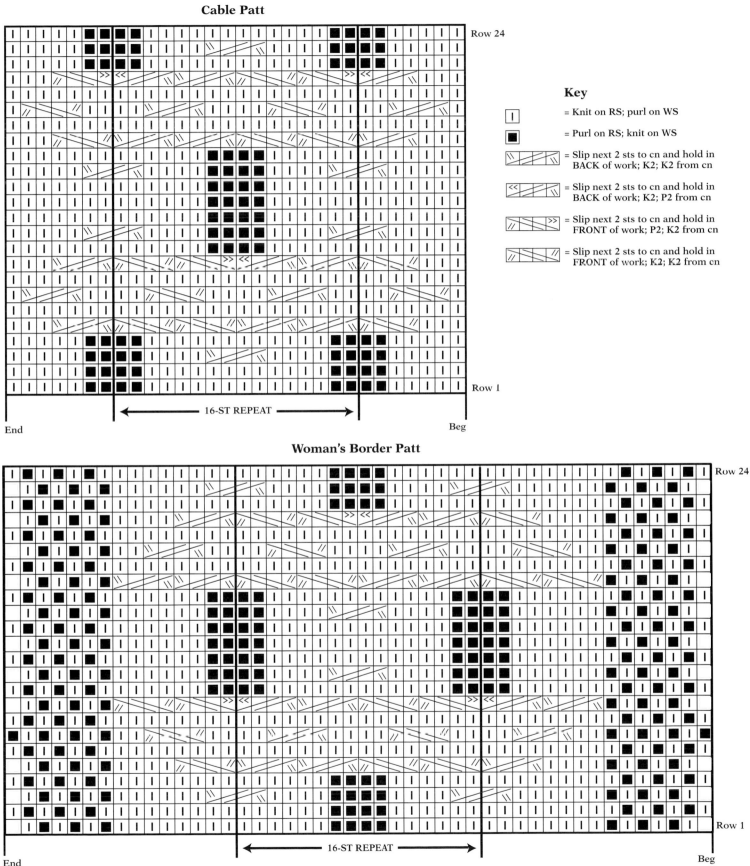

Key

⊔	= Knit on RS; purl on WS
■	= Purl on RS; knit on WS
⟍⟍⟋	= Slip next 2 sts to cn and hold in BACK of work; K2; K2 from cn
≪⟋	= Slip next 2 sts to cn and hold in BACK of work; K2; P2 from cn
⟋≫	= Slip next 2 sts to cn and hold in FRONT of work; P2; K2 from cn
⟋⟋	= Slip next 2 sts to cn and hold in FRONT of work; K2; K2 from cn

16-ST REPEAT

End   Beg

Woman's Border Patt

16-ST REPEAT

End   Beg

Man's Crew-Neck Pullover

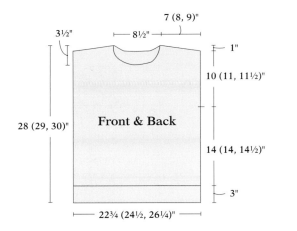

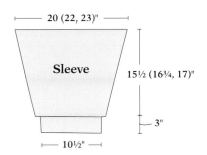

Skill Level
Intermediate

Sizes
Man's Small (Medium, Large). Instructions are for smallest size, with changes for other sizes noted in parentheses as necessary.

Finished Measurements
Chest: 45½ (49, 52½)"/115.5 (124.5, 133.5) cm
Length: 28 (29, 30)"/71 (73.5, 76) cm
Sleeve width at upper arm: 20 (22, 23)"/51 (56, 58.5) cm

Materials
♦ Unique Kolours/Cynthia Helene's *Merino DK 8-ply* (sport weight; 100% wool; 1¾ oz/50 g; approx 123 yds/113 m), 25 (26, 28) balls Prairie #178

♦ Knitting needles, sizes 4 and 6 (3.5 and 4 mm) or size needed to obtain gauge
♦ 16"/40 cm circular knitting needle, size 4 (3.5 mm)
♦ Two stitch holders
♦ Cable needle

Gauge
With larger needles in Cable Patt, 36 sts and 32 rows = 4"/10 cm. **To save time, take time to check gauge.**

Back
With smaller needles, CO 206 (222, 238) sts. Work Man's Border Patt Rows 1 to 4 until piece measures 3"/7.5 cm from beg, ending after Row 4 of patt. Work Rows 5 to 8 of chart once. Change to larger needles and work Cable Patt until piece measures 27 (28, 29)"/68.5 (71, 73.5) cm from beg.
Shape Neck and Shoulders: BO 16 (18, 20) sts at beg of next six rows, 17 (19, 21) sts at beg of next two rows;

and at the same time, slip middle 46 sts onto holder for back of neck; and working both sides at once with separate balls of yarn, BO 5 sts each neck edge three times.

Front
Work same as back until piece measures 24½ (25½, 26½)"/62 (65, 67.5) cm from beg.
Shape Neck: Work across first 88 (96, 104) sts, slip middle 30 sts onto holder for front of neck; join second ball of yarn and work to end row. Work both sides at once with separate balls of yarn, and BO from each neck edge 5 sts once, 4 sts twice, 3 sts twice, 2 sts once, then dec 1 st each neck edge every row twice; **and at the same time,** when front measures same as back to shoulders, **Shape Shoulders** same as for back.

Key

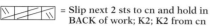 = Knit on RS; purl on WS

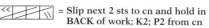 = Purl on RS; knit on WS

= Slip next 2 sts to cn and hold in BACK of work; K2; K2 from cn

= Slip next 2 sts to cn and hold in BACK of work; K2; P2 from cn

= Slip next 2 sts to cn and hold in FRONT of work; P2; K2 from cn

= Slip next 2 sts to cn and hold in FRONT of work; K2; K2 from cn

Man's Border Patt

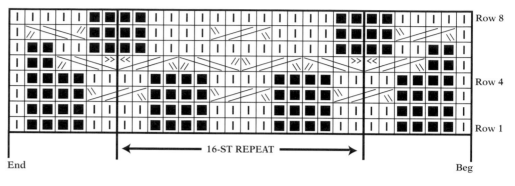

← 16-ST REPEAT →

End   Beg

Sleeves

With smaller needles, CO 94 sts. Work Man's Border Patt Rows 1 to 4 until piece measures 3"/7.5 cm from beg, ending after Row 4 of patt. Work Rows 5 to 8 of chart once. Change to larger needles and beg Cable Patt. Inc 1 st each side every other row 28 (41, 50) times, then every fourth row 15 (11, 7) times—180 (198, 208) sts. Cont even until sleeve measures 18½ (19¾, 20)"/47 (50, 51) cm from beg. BO.

Finishing

Sew shoulder seams.
Neckband: With RS facing and circular knitting needle, pick up and knit 168 sts around neckline, including sts from neck holders. Work as follows: Rnds 1, 2, and 4: *P2, K4, P2; repeat from * around. Rnd 3: *P2, Slip 2 sts to cn and hold in **back** of work; K2, K2 from cn, P2; repeat from * around. Repeat Rnds 1 to 4 for 1"/2.5 cm, ending after Rnd 3 of patt. Next Rnd: Work Rnd 4 and BO.
Place markers 10 (11, 11½)"/25.5 (28, 29) cm down from shoulders. Set in sleeves between markers. Sew sleeve and side seams.

Child's Medallion Crew-Neck Pullover

Skill Level
Expert

Sizes
Child's size 8 (10, 12, 14). Instructions are for smallest size, with changes for other sizes noted in parentheses as necessary.

Finished Measurements
Chest: 35 (36, 39, 40)"/89 (91.5, 99, 101.5) cm

Length: 18 (19, 20, 21)"/45.5 (48.5, 51, 53.5) cm

Sleeve width at upper arm: 16 (16, 17, 18)"/40.5 (40.5, 43, 45.5) cm

Materials
- Unique Kolours/Cynthia Helene's *Merino DK 8-ply* (sport weight; 100% wool; 1¾ oz/50 g; approx 123 yds/113 m), 12 (13, 14, 15) balls Heather #267
- Knitting needles, sizes 4 and 6 (3.5 and 4 mm) or size needed to obtain gauge
- 16"/40 cm circular knitting needle, size 4 (3.5 mm)
- Two stitch holders
- Cable needle

Gauge
With larger needles in Seed St, 24 sts and 36 rows = 4". **To save time, take time to check gauge.**

Child's Medallion Crew-Neck Pullover

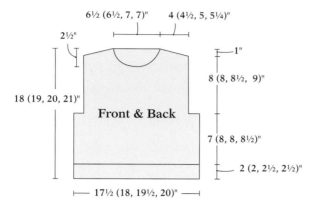

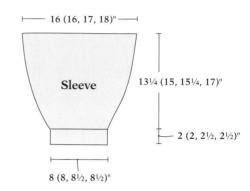

Seed St
Same as for Woman's Tunic.

Back
With smaller needles, CO 105 (109, 117, 121) sts. Work K1 P1 rib for 2 (2, 2½, 2½)"/5 (5, 6.5, 6.5) cm. Change to larger needles, and work Seed St until piece measures 9 (10, 10½, 11)"/23 (25.5, 26.5, 28) cm from beg.
Shape Armholes: BO 8 sts at beg of next two rows—89 (93, 101, 105) sts rem. Cont even until piece measures 17 (18, 19, 20)"/43 (45.5, 48.5, 51) cm from beg.
Shape Shoulders: BO 6 (7, 7, 8) sts at beg of next six rows, then BO 7 (6, 8, 7) sts at beg of next two rows. Slip rem 39 (39, 43, 43) sts onto holder for back of neck.

Front
Work same as back until piece measures 6 (7, 7½, 8)"/15 (18, 19, 20.5) cm from beg.

Beg Medallion: Work across first 38 (40, 44, 46) sts, work Row 1 of Medallion Patt over middle 29 sts, work to end row. Cont in Seed St with Medallion Patt in center of front, working inc and dec as shown in chart; **and at the same time,** when piece measures same as back to underarm, **Shape Armholes** same as for back.
When Row 72 of chart is completed, cont even in Seed St until piece measures 15½ (16½, 17½, 18½)"/39.5 (42, 44.5, 47) cm from beg.
Shape Neck: Work across first 37 (39, 42, 44) sts, slip middle 15 (15, 17, 17) sts onto holder for front of neck; join second ball of yarn and work to end row. Work both sides at once with separate balls of yarn, and BO 4 sts each neck edge once, BO 3 sts each neck edge once, BO 2 sts each neck edge once, then dec 1 st each neck edge every other row 3 (3, 4, 4) times; **and at the same time,** when front measures same as back to shoulders, **Shape Shoulders** same as for back.

Sleeves
With smaller needles, CO 49 (49, 51, 51) sts. Work K1 P1 rib for 2 (2, 2½, 2½)"/5 (5, 6.5, 6.5) cm. Change to larger needles, beg Seed St, and inc 1 st each side every fourth row 18 (10, 15, 16) times, then every sixth row 6 (14, 11, 13) times—97 (97, 103, 109) sts. Cont even until sleeve measures 15¼ (17, 17¾, 19½)"/38.5 (43, 45, 49.5) cm from beg. BO.

Finishing
Sew shoulder seams.
Neckband: With RS facing and circular knitting needle, pick up and K96 (96, 102, 102) around neckline, including sts from neck holders. Work rnds of K1 P1 rib for 2"/5 cm. Work Stockinette St for seven rnds, decreasing 12 sts evenly along first rnd—84 (84, 90, 90) sts rem. BO **loosely.**
Set in sleeves. Sew sleeve and side seams.

Key

■ = St which does not exist yet

| = Knit on RS; purl on WS

■ = Purl on WS; knit on WS

▼ = Make 3 sts out of 1 st: Knit into the BACK and then knit into the FRONT of st; then insert LH needle behind the same st and pick up the vertical strand there and knit into the BACK of it

∨ = Make 2 sts out of 1 st: Knit into the BACK and then knit into the FRONT of st

╱ = k2tog

▲ = Slip 3 sts with yarn in BACK; *pass second st on RH needle over the first st; slip this center st back to LH needle and pass the second st on LH needle over it; slip the center st back to RH needle and repeat from * again; then knit the remaining center st

╱ = p2tog

╲ = ssk

= Slip next st to cn and hold in BACK of work; K3; knit st on cn in the row below; knit the same st on cn the regular way

= Slip next 3 sts to cn and hold in FRONT of work; knit next st in the row below; knit into same st the regular way; K3 from cn

= Slip next 2 sts to cn and hold in BACK of work; K2; P2 from cn

= Slip next 2 sts to cn and hold in FRONT of work; P2; K2 from cn

= Slip next to cn and hold in BACK of work; K3; knit st from cn

= Slip next 3 sts to cn and hold in FRONT of work; knit next st; K3 from cn

= K2; knit next st in the row below; then knit it in the regular way

= Knit into next st in the row below; then knit it in the regular way; K2

= Slip next 2 sts to cn and hold in BACK of work; K3; K2 from cn

= Slip next 3 sts to cn and hold in FRONT of work; K2; K3 from cn

= Slip next 3 sts to cn and hold in BACK of work; K3; K3 from cn

= Slip next 3 sts to cn and hold in FRONT of work; K3; K3 from cn

= Slip next 2 sts to cn and hold in FRONT of work; K2; K2 from cn

= Slip next 2 sts to cn and hold in BACK of work; K2; K2 from cn

= Slip next 3 sts to cn and hold in FRONT of work; p2tog; K3 from cn

= Slip next 2 sts to cn and hold in BACK of work; K3; p2tog from cn

= Slip next 3 sts to cn and hold in FRONT of work; k2tog; K3 from cn

= Slip next 2 sts to cn and hold in BACK of work; K3; k2tog from cn

= Slip next 3 sts to cn and hold in FRONT of work; purl next st; K3 from cn

= Slip next st to cn and hold in BACK of work; K3; purl st from cn

Medallion Patt

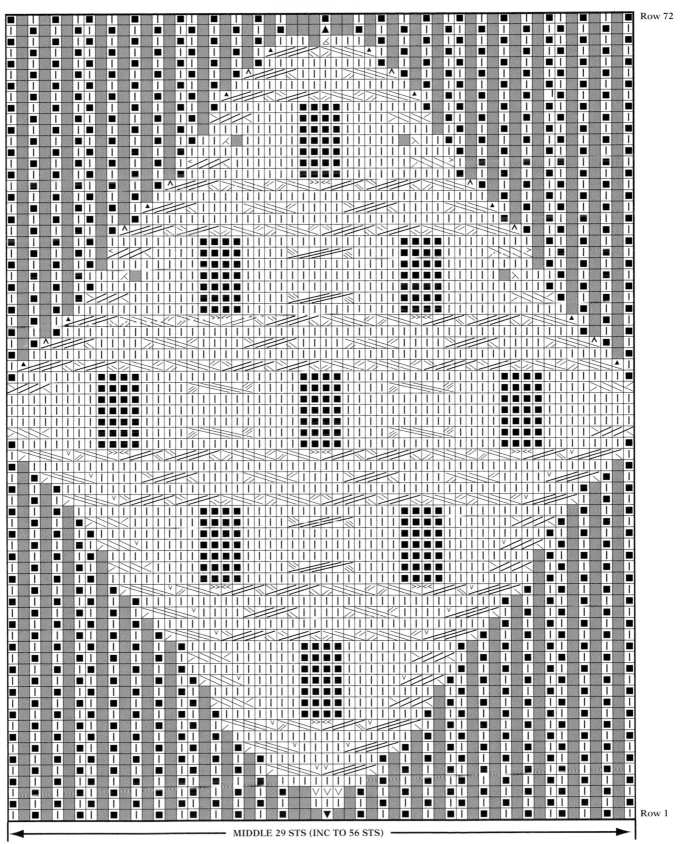

Row 72

Row 1

MIDDLE 29 STS (INC TO 56 STS)

Casual Comfort

Terrific shapes and textures combine to create
this wearable sporty trio. Seed Stitch provides
the perfect ground for cables. Each cable
is slightly different from the others, ensuring
that these projects will be interesting and
fun to knit.

Woman's High-Neck Pullover

Designer Hint

Shaped shoulders allow sweaters to hang naturally along the body, but binding off in stages can create problems when sewing shoulders together. To avoid those stair steps, slip the first stitch of each set, then bind off as usual.

Skill Level

Intermediate

Sizes

Woman's Small (Medium, Large, Extra-Large). Instructions are for smallest size, with changes for other sizes noted in parentheses as necessary.

Finished Measurements

Bust: 36½ (40, 44½, 49)"/92.5 (101.5, 113, 124.5) cm

Length: 19½ (20½, 20½, 21½)"/50 (52, 52, 54.5) cm

Sleeve width at upper arm: 13 (14, 15, 15)"/33 (35.5, 38, 38) cm

Materials

- Lion Brand's *Wool-Ease* (worsted weight; 80% acrylic/20% wool; 3 oz/85 g; approx 197 yds/177 m), 7 (7, 8, 8) skeins Dark Rose Heather #139
- Knitting needles, sizes 6 and 7 (4 and 4.5 mm) or size needed to obtain gauge
- 16"/40 cm circular knitting needle, size 6 (4 mm)
- Cable needle

Gauge

With larger needles in Seed St, 20 sts and 34 rows = 4"/10 cm. **To save time, take time to check gauge.**

Seed St (over odd number of sts)

Row 1 (RS): *K1, P1. Repeat from * across, ending row with K1.

Row 2: Work same as Row 1.

Repeat Rows 1 and 2 for patt.

Back

With smaller needles, CO 100 (108, 116, 128) sts. Work K1 P1 rib for 2"/5 cm. Next Row (RS): Change to larger needles, and work first 31 (35, 39, 45) sts in Seed St, place marker, work Row 1 of Woman's Cable Patt over next 38 sts, place marker, work Seed St to end row. Cont in patt as established and inc 1 st each side (working inc sts into Seed St) every tenth row 0 (0, 5, 4) times, every twelfth row 0 (0, 1, 2) times, every fourteenth row 3 (1, 0, 0) times, then every eighteenth row 1 (3, 0, 0) times—108 (116, 128, 140) sts. Work even until piece measures 10½ (11, 10½, 11½)"/26.5 (28, 26.5, 29) cm from beg.

Shape Armholes: BO 4 sts at beg of next two rows, then BO 2 sts at beg of next two rows. Dec 1 st each side every other row 1 (3, 9, 14) times, then every fourth row 3 (3, 1, 0) times—88 (92, 96, 100) sts rem. Cont even until armholes measure 8 (8½, 9, 9)"/20.5 (21.5, 23, 23) cm.

Shape Shoulders: BO 4 (5, 6, 4) sts at beg of next four rows, then BO 3 (3, 3, 5) sts at beg of next six rows. BO rem 54 sts.

Front

Work same as back until armholes measure 6¾ (7¼, 7¾, 7¾)"/17 (18.5, 19.5, 19.5) cm.

Shape Neck: Work across first 29 (31, 33, 35) sts; join second skein of yarn and BO middle 30 sts, work to end of row. Work both sides at once with

Woman's High-Neck Pullover

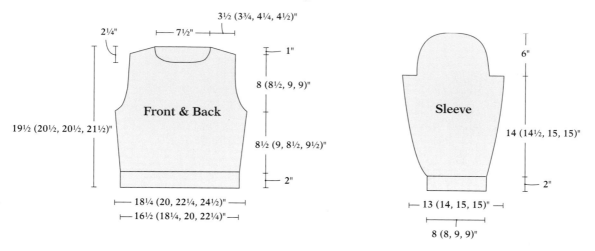

separate skeins of yarn, and BO 3 sts each neck edge once, BO 2 sts each neck edge twice, then dec 1 st each neck edge every other row five times; **and at the same time,** when front measures same as back to shoulders, **Shape Shoulders** same as for back.

Sleeves

With smaller needles, CO 41 (41, 47, 47) sts. Work K1 P1 rib for 2"/5 cm. Next Row: Change to larger needles, beg Seed St, and inc 1 st each side every sixth row 0 (7, 1, 1) times, then every eighth row 13 (9, 14, 14) times—67 (73, 77, 77) sts. Cont even until sleeve measures 16 (16½, 17, 17)"/40.5 (42, 43, 43) cm from beg.

Shape Cap: BO 4 sts at beg of next two rows, then dec 1 st each side every fourth row 10 (7, 7, 7) times, then every other row 3 (9, 9, 9) times. BO 3 sts at beg of next four rows. BO rem 21 (21, 25, 25) sts.

Finishing

Sew shoulder seams.
Neckband: With RS facing and circular knitting needle, pick up and K94 around neckline. Work rnds of K1 P1 rib for 3"/7.5 cm. BO **loosely** in rib. Set in sleeves. Sew sleeve and side seams.

Key

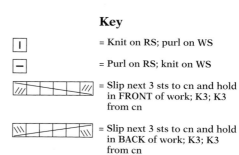

I	= Knit on RS; purl on WS
−	= Purl on RS; knit on WS
/// ///	= Slip next 3 sts to cn and hold in FRONT of work; K3; K3 from cn
\\\ \\\	= Slip next 3 sts to cn and hold in BACK of work; K3; K3 from cn

Woman's Cable Patt

Row 8

Row 1

38 STS

Man's Zippered Pullover

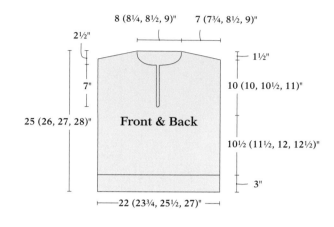

8 (8¼, 8½, 9)" 7 (7¾, 8½, 9)"

2½"

7"

1½"

10 (10, 10½, 11)"

25 (26, 27, 28)"

Front & Back

10½ (11½, 12, 12½)"

3"

22 (23¾, 25½, 27)"

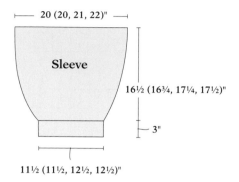

20 (20, 21, 22)"

Sleeve

16½ (16¾, 17¼, 17½)"

3"

11½ (11½, 12½, 12½)"

Skill Level
Intermediate

Sizes
Man's Small (Medium, Large, Extra-Large). Instructions are for smallest size, with changes for other sizes noted in parentheses as necessary.

Finished Measurements
Chest: 44 (47½, 51, 54)"/112 (120.5, 129.5, 137) cm

Length: 25 (26, 27, 28)"/63.5 (66, 68.5, 71) cm

Sleeve width at upper arm: 20 (20, 21, 22)"/51 (51, 53.5, 56) cm

Materials
♦ Lion Brand's *Wool-Ease* (worsted weight; 80% acrylic/20% wool; 3 oz/85 g; approx 197 yds/177 m), 10 (10, 11, 12) skeins Blue Heather #107

♦ Knitting needles, sizes 6 and 7 (4 and 4.5 mm) or size needed to obtain gauge
♦ Cable needle
♦ One stitch holder
♦ One safety pin
♦ 7"/18 cm zipper

Gauge
With larger needles in Seed St, 20 sts and 34 rows = 4"/10 cm. **To save time, take time to check gauge.**

Seed St
Same as for Woman's High-Neck Pullover.

Back
With smaller needles, CO 129 (137, 145, 153) sts. Work K1 P1 rib for 3"/7.5 cm. Next Row (RS): Change to larger needles, work first 23 (27, 31, 35) sts in Seed St, place marker, work Row 1 of Man's Cable Patt over next 20 sts, place marker, work Seed St over middle 43 sts, place marker, work Row 1 Man's Cable Patt over next 20 sts, place marker, work Seed St to end row. Cont in patt as established until piece measures 23½ (24½, 25½, 26½)"/59.5 (62, 65, 67.5) cm from beg.

Shape Shoulders: BO 7 (8, 8, 9) sts at beg of next six rows, then BO 8 (8, 9, 9) sts at beg of next six rows. Slip rem 39 (41, 43, 45) sts onto holder for back of neck.

Man's Cable Patt

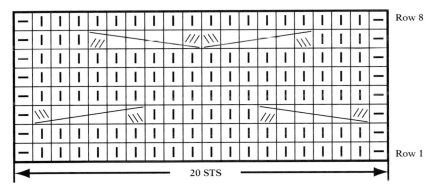

Row 8

Row 1

← 20 STS →

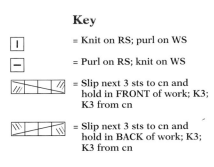

Key

☐ = Knit on RS; purl on WS

☐ = Purl on RS; knit on WS

= Slip next 3 sts to cn and hold in FRONT of work; K3; K3 from cn

= Slip next 3 sts to cn and hold in BACK of work; K3; K3 from cn

Front

Work same as back until piece measures 15½ (16½, 17½, 18½)"/39.5 (42, 44.5, 47) cm from beg.

Divide for Zipper Opening: Work across first 63 (67, 71, 75) sts, slip middle 3 sts onto safety pin for bottom of zipper placket; join second skein of yarn and work to cnd row. Work both sides at once with separate skeins of yarn until piece measures 22½ (23½, 24½, 25½)"57 (59.5, 62, 65) cm from the beg.

Shape Neck: BO 4 sts each neck edge once (twice, twice, twice), BO 3 sts each neck edge twice (once, once, twice), BO 2 sts each neck edge twice, then dec 1 st each neck edge every other row 4 (4, 5, 3) times; **and at the same time,** when piece measures same as back to shoulders, **Shape Shoulders** same as for back.

Sleeves

With smaller needles, CO 59 (59, 65, 65) sts. Work K1 P1 rib for 3"/7.5 cm. Next Row: Change to larger needles, beg Seed St, and inc 1 st each side every sixth row 19 (18, 15, 22) times, then every eighth row 2 (3, 6, 1) times—101 (101, 107, 111) sts. Cont even until sleeve measures 19½ (19¾, 20¼, 20½)"/49.5 (50, 51.5, 52) cm from beg. BO.

Finishing

Sew shoulder seams.

Collar: With RS facing and smaller needles, pick up and K93 (97, 101, 105) around neckline, including sts from back neck holder. Work K1 P1 rib for 1"/2.5 cm. Next Row: Change to larger needles, and inc 1 st at beg and end of row. Cont even in rib until collar measures 2"/5 cm from beg. Next Row: Cont in rib, and inc 1 st at beg and end of row. Cont even until collar measures 3"/7.5 cm from beg. BO in rib.

Placket Edging: With smaller needles, pick up and K41 along right edge of placket, 3 sts from safety pin, and 41 sts along left edge of placket—85 sts total. Next Row: Knit to BO. Sew in zipper.

Place markers 10 (10, 10½, 11)"/25.5 (25.5, 26.5, 28) cm down from shoulders. Set in sleeves between markers. Sew sleeve and side seams.

Baby's Cardigan and Pants Set

Skill Level
Intermediate

Sizes
Infant's 6 (12, 18) months. Instructions are written for smallest size, with changes for other sizes noted in parentheses as necessary.

Finished Measurements
Cardigan chest (buttoned): 24½ (26¼, 29½)"/62(66.5, 75) cm
Cardigan length: 11 (12½, 13½)"/28 (32, 34.5) cm
Cardigan sleeve width at upper arm: 9½ (10½, 11½)"/24 (26.5, 29) cm
Pants length: 15 (16, 17)"/38 (40.5, 43) cm

Materials
- Lion Brand's *Wool-Ease* (worsted weight; 80% acrylic/20% wool; 3 oz/85 g; approx 197 yds/177 m), 5 (6, 6) skeins Ivory Sprinkles #097
- Knitting needles, sizes 6 and 7 (4 and 4.5 mm) or size needed to obtain gauge
- 16"/40 cm circular knitting needle, size 6 (4 mm)
- Cable needle
- Two stitch holders
- Five ½"/15 mm buttons (JHB International's *Moonstone* style #71618 in White was used in sample garment)
- 1"/2.5 cm wide elastic measured to fit baby's waist

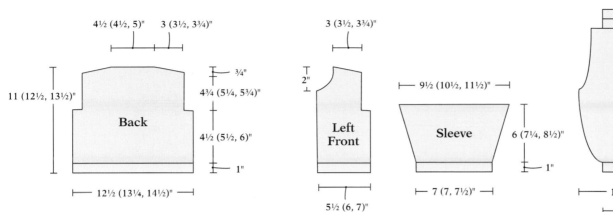

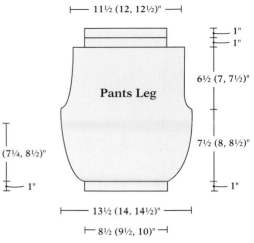

Gauge

With larger needles in Seed St, 20 sts and 34 rows = 4"/10 cm. **To save time, take time to check gauge.**

Seed St

Same as for Woman's High-Neck Pullover.

Cardigan Back

With smaller needles, CO 73 (77, 83) sts. Work K1 P1 rib for 1"/2.5 cm. Next Row (RS): Change to larger needles, work first 11 (13, 15) sts in Seed St, place marker, work Row 1 of Baby's Cable Patt over next 14 sts, place marker, work Seed St over middle 23 (23, 25) sts, place marker, work Row 1 Baby's Cable Patt over next 14 sts, place marker, work Seed St to end of row. Cont in patt as established until piece measures 5½ (6½, 7)"/14 (16.5, 18) cm from beg.

Shape Armholes: BO 5 sts at beg of next two rows—63 (67, 73) sts rem. Cont even until piece measures 10½ (11¾, 12¾)"/26.5 (30, 32.5) cm from the beg.

Shape Shoulders: BO 5 (5, 6) sts at beg of next six rows, then BO 5 (7, 6) sts at beg of next two rows. Slip rem 23 (23, 25) sts onto holder for back of neck.

Cardigan Left Front

With smaller needles, CO 34 (36, 40) sts. Work K1 P1 rib for 1"/2.5 cm. Next Row (RS): Change to larger needles, work first 11 (13, 15) sts in Seed St, place marker, work Row 1 of Baby's Cable Patt over next 14 sts, place marker, work Seed St to end row. Cont in patt as established until piece measures 5½ (6½, 7)"/14 (16.5, 18) cm from beg, ending after WS row.

Shape Armhole: BO 5 sts at beg of next row—29 (31, 35) sts rem. Cont even until piece measures 9 (10½, 11½)"/23 (26.6, 29) cm from beg, ending after RS row.

Shape Neck: BO 2 (2, 3) sts at neck

edge twice, then dec 1 st at neck edge every other row five times; **and at the same time,** when piece measures same as back to shoulders, **Shape Shoulders** same as for back.

Cardigan Right Front

Work same as left front until piece measures 1"/2.5 cm from beg. Next Row (RS): Change to larger needles, work first 9 (9, 11) sts in Seed St, place marker, work Row 1 of Baby's Cable Patt over next 14 sts, place marker, work Seed St to end row. Complete same as left front, *except* reverse all shaping.

Cardigan Sleeves

With smaller needles, CO 35 (35, 37) sts. Work K1 P1 rib for 1"/2.5 cm. Next Row (RS): Change to larger needles, beg Seed St, and inc 1 st each side every fourth row 4 (5, 6) times, then every sixth row 3 (4, 5) times—49 (53, 59) sts. Cont even until sleeve measures 7 (8¼, 9½)"/18 (21, 24) cm from beg. BO.

Baby's Cable Patt

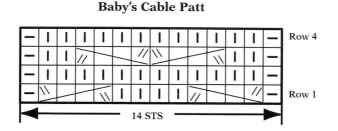

Row 4
Row 1

◄───── 14 STS ─────►

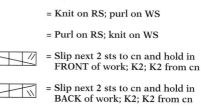

Cardigan Finishing

Sew shoulder seams.

Button Band: With RS facing and smaller needles, pick up and K51 (53, 57) along left front. Work K1 P1 rib for 1"/2.5 cm. BO in rib. Place markers for five evenly spaced buttons along band, making the first ½"/1.5 cm from bottom and the last ½"/1.5 cm from beg of neck shaping.

Buttonhole Band: Work same as for button band, *except* make five buttonholes by working (k2tog, yarn over) opposite markers when band measures ½"/1.5 cm.

Collar: With RS facing and smaller needles, pick up and K51 (51, 53) around neckline, beg and end in center of front bands. Work K1 P1 rib for 1"/2.5 cm. Change to larger needles, and cont in rib, inc 1 st each end every fourth row three times—57 (57, 59) sts total. When collar measures 2½"/6.5 cm from beg, BO **loosely** in rib.
Set in sleeves. Sew sleeve and side seams. Sew on buttons.

Pants Leg (Make Two)

With smaller needles, CO 45 (49, 51) sts. Work K1 P1 rib for 1"/2.5 cm. Change to larger needles, beg Seed St, and inc 1 st each side every fourth row 12 (7, 5) times, then every sixth row 0 (4, 6) times—69 (71, 73) sts. Cont even until piece measures 8½ (9, 9½)"/21.5 (23, 24) cm from beg.

Shape Crotch: BO 2 sts at beg of next two rows, then dec 1 st each side every fourth (fourth, sixth) row 3 (3, 2) times—59 (61, 65) sts. Cont even until piece measures 15 (16, 17)"/38 (40.5, 43) cm from beg. Place sts onto holder.

Pants Finishing

Sew inside leg seams. Sew center front and back seams.

Waistband: With RS facing and circular knitting needle, pick up and knit sts from leg holders. Join, and work rnds of K1 P1 rib for 1"/2.5 cm. Next Rnd (turning ridge): Purl around. Cont rib for 1"/2.5 cm more. BO. Fold waistband in half to WS at turning ridge, and sew it into place to form casing, leaving opening for elastic. Cut elastic to fit waist with ½"/1.5 cm overlap. Slip elastic through casing, and sew ends tog securely. Sew casing closed.

Appendix 1: Yarn Choice and Substitution

Each project in this book was designed for a specific yarn. Different yarns possess their own characteristics that effect the way they appear and behave when knitted. To duplicate the sweaters as photographed, I suggest that you use the designated yarns.

However, if you would like to substitute yarn, be sure to choose one of similar weight to the one called for in the pattern. Knit a test swatch using the needle size recommended on the ball band, making it at least 4"/10 cm square. Measure the number of stitches over 4"/10 cm and use the table below to determine the weight.

Yarn Weight	Stitches per 4"/10 cm
Fingering weight	24 or more
Sport weight	22–24
Light worsted weight	20–22
Worsted weight	19–20
Heavy worsted weight	16–18
Bulky weight	15 or fewer

Appendix 2: Material Resources

Manufacturers

The following companies sell wholesale only. Contact them to locate retail stores in your area.

Brown Sheep Co.
100662 County Rd. 16
Mitchell, NE 69357
(308) 635-2198

Classic Elite
12 Perkins St.
Lowell, MA 01854
(978) 453-2837

Coats/Patons
1001 Roselawn Ave.
Toronto, ON M6B 1B8 Canada
(416) 782-4481

JCA, Inc.
35 Scales Lane
Townsend, MA 01469
(978) 597-8794

JHB International, Inc.
1955 South Quince St.
Denver, CO 80231
(303) 751-8100

Lane Borgosesia
422 E. Vermijo
Colorado Springs, CO 80903
(719) 635-4060

Lion Brand Yarn
34 W. Fifteenth St.
New York, NY 10011
(212) 243-8995

Muench Yarns
285 Bel Marin Keys
Unit J
Novato, CA 94949
(415) 883-6375

Spinrite, Inc.
320 Livingstone Ave. S.
Listowel, ON N4W 3H3 Canada
(519) 291-3780

Tahki Imports, Ltd.
11 Graphic Pl.
Moonachie, NJ 07074
(201) 807-0070

Unique Kolors, Ltd.
1428 Oak Lane
Downingtown, PA 19335
(610) 280-7720

Westminster Fibers
5 Northern Blvd.
Amherst, NH 03031
(603) 886-5041

Mail-Order Sources

Herrschner's Yarn Shoppe
2800 Hoover Rd.
Stevens Point, WI 54492
(800) 441-0838

Patternworks
P.O. Box 1690
Poughkeepsie, NY 12601
(800) 438-5464

Wool Connection
34 E. Main St.
Avon, CT 06001
(800) 933-9665

Appendix 3: Instructional Resources

This book assumes a working knowledge of knitting techniques and includes patterns for a variety of skill levels. For specific technical questions, refer to one of the following books.

Goldberg, Rhoda Ochser. *The New Knitting Dictionary: 1000 Stitches and Patterns.* New York: Crown, 1984.

Mountford, Debra, ed. *The Harmony Guide to Knitting Techniques and Stitches.* New York: Harmony, 1992.

Righetti, Maggie. *Knitting in Plain English.* New York: St. Martins Press, 1986.

Stanley, Montse. *The Reader's Digest Guide to Knitting.* Pleasantville, NY: Reader's Digest, 1993.

Thomas, Mary. *Mary Thomas's Knitting Book.* London: Hodder & Stoughton, Ltd., 1943. Reprint, New York: Dover, 1973.

Vogue Knitting Editors. *Vogue Knitting: The Ultimate Knitting Book.* New York: Pantheon, 1989.

Look for these and other Taunton Press titles at your local bookstore. You can order them direct by calling (800) 888-8286 or by visiting our website at www.taunton.com. Call for a free catalog.

- *Fabric Savvy*
- *Scarves to Make*
- *Fine Embellishment Techniques*
- *Just Pockets*
- *Sew the New Fleece*
- *The Sewing Machine Guide*
- *Fine Machine Sewing*
- *50 Heirloom Buttons to Make*
- *Couture Sewing Techniques*
- *Shirtmaking*
- *Beyond the Pattern*
- *Distinctive Details*
- *Fit and Fabric*
- *Fitting Solutions*
- *Fitting Your Figure*
- *Great Quilting Techniques*
- *Great Sewn Clothes*
- *Jackets, Coats and Suits*
- *Quilts and Quilting*
- *Sewing Tips & Trade Secrets*
- *Stitchery and Needle Lace*

- *Techniques for Casual Clothes*
- *Ribbon Knits*
- *The Jean Moss Book of World Knits*
- *The Knit Hat Book*
- *Knitted Sweater Style*
- *Knitting Tips and Trade Secrets*
- *Hand-Manipulated Stitches for Machine Knitters*
- *Alice Starmore's Book of Fair Isle Knitting*
- *Great Knits*
- *Hand-Knitting Techniques*
- *Knitting Around the World*
- *Colorful Knitwear Design*
- *American Country Needlepoint*

Sewing Companion Library:
- *Easy Guide to Serging Fine Fabrics*
- *Easy Guide to Sewing Blouses*
- *Easy Guide to Sewing Jackets*
- *Easy Guide to Sewing Linings*
- *Easy Guide to Sewing Pants*
- *Easy Guide to Sewing Skirts*
- *Easy Guide to Sewing Tops & T-Shirts*